Triumph Against Trouble

Other Books by W. Phillip Keller

God Is My Delight
Joshua: Mighty Warrior and Man of Faith
Outdoor Moments with God
Sky Edge: Mountaintop Meditations
Songs of My Soul: Daily Devotions from the Writings of Phillip Keller
Strength of Soul: The Sacred Use of Time
Wonder O' the Wind

Triumph Against Trouble

Finding God's Power in Life's Problems

W. PHILLIP KELLER

Grand Rapids, MI 49501

Triumph Against Trouble

Published by Kregel Publications, a division of Kregel, Inc., P.O. Box 2607, Grand Rapids, MI 49501. Kregel Publications provides trusted, biblical publications for Christian growth and service. Your comments and suggestions are valued.

Cover design: Alan G. Hartman
Book design: Nicholas G. Richardson

Library of Congress Cataloging-in-Publication Data
Keller, W. Phillip (Weldon Phillip), 1920–
Triumph against trouble / W. Phillip Keller.
p. cm.
1. Christian life. 2. Suffering—Religious aspects—Christianity. 3. Keller, W. Phillip (Weldon Phillip).
I. Title.
BV4501.2K4259 1995 248.8'6—dc20 95-16952
CIP

ISBN 0-8254-2994-3

1 2 3 4 5 printing/year 00 99 98 97 96

Printed in the United States of America

To those dear, dear friends
who in our time of trouble
showed so much love and kindness,
always!

Table of Contents

Acknowledgments

No book of this sort is ever the work of just one person. It reaches out to touch and embrace all others who had a part in its events.

Of these, Cheri, my wife, was such a sturdy and courageous companion. We faced this time of trouble together. It was tough for her just as it was tough for me. We shared in the trials and tears as well as in the triumphs.

Together we have given humble but hearty thanks to our Father for sustaining us with His care. He has been our Strength, our Hope, our Deliverer.

We here express genuine gratitude to those dear, dear friends who came to us in our distress, who poured out their affection upon us in abundant measure, and who helped us in such practical ways.

Our profound appreciation goes out to Fern Webber, long-time friend, who has the skill to turn my handwritten work into a proper manuscript.

Nor would I forget the precious people who pray for me every morning. Truly Christ Himself has honored their petitions for throughout this entire endeavor, He has been present in wondrous reality to guide the work and inspire my own soul.

W. PHILLIP KELLER

The Background of This Book

This morning, in the early dawn light, heavy dark clouds swirl through the overcast. The whole earth appears dark, forbidding, yes, almost frightening. Seldom do our hills, our forests, and our mountain glades seem stained with such black hues. An atmosphere of despair and discouragement encompasses all I can see—all the earth around me seems depressed.

But, within the warm walls of my study there is the intense, bright light of several beautiful light fixtures—one on my desk, its glow flooding this paper, another on the ceiling, splashing its radiance into every corner.

Darkness without!

Brightness within!

That is the story of this book. It is a simple account of one man's confrontation with trouble heaped upon trouble yet amid the turmoil finding the pervasive Presence of the Living Christ within, to cheer, to sustain, and to overcome.

This narration of God's gracious generosity in the face of so many difficulties and apparent reverses is written to help others discover His hand in all of their adversities. It is very easy for Christians to exult in God's goodness when things go well. But there arise great dark doubts when things go wrong.

Often, people earnestly wonder if they have stepped outside the Father's will for them, or they may feel like He has abandoned them in trouble. Some go so far as to insist that they are the victims of the Enemy's (Satan's) sinister schemes.

This book, in simple language anyone can understand, recounts how the child of God can triumph against trouble. In the center of every crisis, we can know and rest in the presence of Christ.

For five long, trying months, beginning in the fall of 1993, difficulty upon difficulty dogged our steps. As sometimes happens in life, trouble came in tangled knots. One adversity would just be resolved only to be swiftly followed by another. There seemed to be no end in sight, especially as my own health and well-being drastically deteriorated.

There were days when I was so weak, so spent, so exhausted that in childlike earnestness I asked my Father in glory if my days on earth were done. Was my earthly existence at an end? Was it the end of our great adventure together on this planet? Was He about to call me "home"?

As it turned out, that was not to be the case!

Our glorious Father had surprising purposes in all the difficulties that I faced. He intended that I should be restored, and he was determined that I should triumph against trouble.

Then on a gentle spring day, alone on a sun-splashed beach, my strength renewed, I asked Him, "O living Lord Jesus Christ, what do you wish me to do now?"

It was a simple, sincere, straightforward request with no preconditions.

I wanted just to do His bidding.

In the supreme stillness of that secluded shore, the inner, immediate assurance that came to me clearly from Him was: *Go home in peace. Declare My generosity to you in all your trouble. Write a moving memorial to Me, stating how My presence has preserved you!*

Pure joy, ecstatic enthusiasm, and abundant energy from the Most High swept through all my being—body, soul, mind, and spirit. All was well within!

That day at dawn this work began with Him. May it endure not only to enrich and uplift all who read it but also to honor Him who is sovereign in heaven and earth.

Chapter One

Injured Knees

This story begins in such an innocent way. Like so many difficult days, my adversity came without warning. It just happened in stillness and in silence. All summer I had been fit, well, and strong. September had been a glorious month, inviting me, as it does every year, to climb the hills, explore the high ridges, and roam free in company with the bear, deer, coyotes, and wild sheep of our northern mountains.

But this golden autumn it was not to be. Suddenly all those high-country days were done. I was a maimed "mountain man."

I had awakened at dawn on a cool October morning. I was not camped out in the hills. I was in my own warm bed at home. Suddenly my right thigh was gripped as in a vise by the excruciating pain of a common charley horse. The stout, strong thigh muscles knotted up until they could knot no further.

At first, I attempted to rub and massage them back into place. But this procedure, simple and effective as it had been before, brought no relief. In agony I writhed on the bed, gasping for relief.

Foolishly, in a frantic impulse to free my muscles from this searing spasm, I kicked out violently. There was an ominous, dull tearing sound in my knee. Suddenly stabbing pain shot through it and down into my calf.

It was a serious, self-inflicted injury that in a matter of moments crippled me. Because of a drastic accident to my other knee as a boy, I knew in the darkness of that dawn that I faced a formidable fight to recover. I knew that only Christ's supernatural help could heal me.

The incident recounted here is not to elicit special sympathy from the reader nor to press any point of view about our Father's capacity to heal injuries. It is told to explain how it is possible to have great peace within in order to withstand great pain without.

As I dressed myself that morning, standing stiffly on my left leg like an awkward stork, vivid memories of my other injured knee swept across my memory. In one way the memories dismayed me because the injuries had cost me so much pain and suffering. Yet, at the same time they brought back a calm assurance that God is faithful. He had restored me before and He could heal me again—even though I was now an elderly man.

My first knee injury was to the left one. I was a lad of fifteen in a tough boys only school 250 miles away from home. On the sports field we were taught to play ruthlessly, without giving ground to the opponent. In a vicious, hot-blooded game of field hockey an attacker smashed his heavy stick full force across my left knee. The kneecap shattered, and I dropped to the ground as if struck by a .303 rifle bullet.

The closest doctor was miles away in Nairobi, Kenya. By the time I was carried to his clinic my left leg had swollen to twice its normal size. We wore no protective padding, so the full impact of my opponent's mighty slash had made a serious mess of my knee.

At best, British doctors are a patient, calm fraternity. But this dear old practitioner took a careful look at the shattered joint and stated quietly, "Son, I fear you will never, ever walk normally again!"

Now, not only was my knee shattered, so were my hopes. I was an unusually energetic, active boy, but my legs were my special strength—for running, climbing, hiking, and exploring all the wide wilderness that I loved so fiercely. Was I to be a cripple the rest of my life? Would I have to hobble around on crutches, only half a person? The very thought made me mad with rage until my blood boiled in my veins.

Then and there I was determined to beat this thing.

I refused to accept the doctor's dim verdict.

In almost defiant faith I knew I could win.

In those far-off days, almost sixty years ago, I had seen first-hand the remarkable recovery made by so many Africans who came to Mother and Dad for help and healing. My parents were not medical people. They were layworkers with the mission who ran a small dispensary where simple remedies like castor oil, quinine, and iodine were issued to suffering patients. But far and beyond this was their unshakable calm, quiet trust in Christ to cure complicated conditions and to heal massive injuries. And He simply did this for them, as He had done by the Sea of Galilee so long ago.

So, what I had seen at home, I somehow felt sure I could see at school in my own dilemma. Not that I claim to have had any great faith in God at that time in my life. Simply put, I was a rough, tough kid who was sure Christ could heal me.

The old doctor sent me away with a package of long elastic bandages, a large jar of anti-inflammatory cream, and stern orders to keep my knee packed with the claylike substance. Somehow he seemed to feel that any other remedies were futile.

But I did not. With My Lord's help I would walk again. For months and months I packed that grotesque knee. Bit by bit it began to mend. Then one day I walked bravely.

Since that memorable morning until this very day, some sixty years later, I had walked, run, hiked, climbed mountains, and played tennis on that terrible knee. So, as I stood there awkwardly pulling on my pants, I knew as of old that what Christ had accomplished then, He could accomplish again. Amid the darkness was light—His light!

What I did not know was just how the healing would happen. I had no clear idea of how I would come to walk normally again. I would have to wait to see. But above all, within me there was a calm, quiet, unshakable assurance that all would be well. I would walk again with vigor, freedom, and strength no matter how much I limped on this lame leg now. My confidence was not in my own physical condition but in my Father's wondrous ways to help and to heal.

In sincerity and integrity I would do my part.

Likewise in humility and earnestness I would trust Him to do His part.

Between us we would beat this thing and honor Him.

This was in fact to triumph against trouble.

The well-meaning friends and neighbors whom I met during my short, painful little walks around the garden and along the mailbox road were hardly a help. I say this not in criticism but as a commentary on how Christian culture deals with disease and bodily injuries like mine.

I know two elderly men, one about my age, the other a little older, who had both damaged the same joint as I had. Straightway both of them had rushed off to their respective doctors for counsel. Both of them were referred on to bone specialists. Both agreed to submit to massive surgery. Both, by their choices, demonstrated not only that their faith lay in medical science but also in the ability of our system to pay the enormous costs.

One of them met me hobbling along under the graceful limbs of some golden white-bark birches along the road. I had paused to admire the glorious foliage flung in wild abandon against the blue October sky.

"What's up?" he asked rather gruffly.

Without going into any details I replied, "Just an injured knee."

He looked at me sternly and said, "Old man, you hardly need that at your age. Better see a specialist at once!" And with a grin he was gone.

What he said was true.

But the solution he offered did not sit well with me—especially since he was regarded as one of the most prominent Christian leaders in our community.

Within my own spirit I turned calmly to Christ. Then I spoke softly in hushed tones, "O my Master, You have not changed across the centuries. You can restore my strength. You are the Beloved Physician who can renew my injured knee."

A quiet peace pervaded my whole person.

A calm assurance enfolded my soul.

All was well within—even though I still stumbled up the rough country lane to the mailbox.

One lesson that I had learned long ago in sharing life with the Father was to not rush things, not to demand instant results, but to learn to wait quietly for Him to set the stage and direct the drama of my days.

This had not been an easy lesson. By nature I am a man of action—my personality, so impatient and so exacting, wants to see things done—delays are difficult! But, little by little, step-by-step, in childlike confidence I am learning to wait *for God to act* on my behalf.

Waiting for God to act is a supreme spiritual secret in walking with Him. It does not come to us in some stirring vision overnight. It comes softly day by day, as we walk gently with Him in the way.

> But they that wait upon the LORD shall renew their strength; they shall mount up with wings as eagles; they shall run, and not be weary; and they shall walk, and not faint (Isa. 40:31).

We have all heard this verse a hundred times. We claim to believe it, yet we turn to human technology for help. We demand that doctors do something drastic. We simply will not wait for God's good time.

But, stubborn old mountain man that I am, I was determined to wait as I had over and over and over since I was thirty-four years of age. When the doctors had given me up to die, I learned to wait for my Father to heal me. In His bountiful mercy and generous grace He had restored me many times—from blindness, from a massive heart attack, from so-called incurable conditions. For over thirty-two years I had not even had a medical check-up. Of course He could renew me again if He so chose.

Yes, yes I would wait even if others scoffed facetiously.

I would wait even if friends called me a fanatic.

I would wait even if my associates thought me a fool.

It would not be easy!

At the time, I was teaching a series of Bible studies in a

town fifty miles north of our home. Week after week I endured the agony of driving to and fro in heavy traffic. En route I had to climb out of the car and exercise the injured joint to get relief. I had to hobble up to the platform to speak, then stand there perched on my left leg. After one and one-half hours, I was spent but still had to drive home.

Deliberately, I made every effort to mask my awkward movements. I did not want sympathy. I did not want scores of well-wishers sending me off to their specialists. I did not want to become some sort of sensation.

My injured knee was a private, personal issue between my Father and me.

Time in His hands has a way of resolving difficulties.

October, under warm Indian summer skies, drifted on.

A year earlier, arrangements had been made for us to spend a few days at one of our favorite hideaways in the Rockies. Purposely we had planned to be there when the fall foliage turned gold and crimson. But this year would be so different because of my bum knee—very little hiking, and certainly no climbing in the high ranges.

Then a startling thought swept into my consciousness: *Go up and soak, soak, stretch, stretch, and exercise, exercise your body in those warm hot springs that gush from the rocks.* The idea electrified me! There was healing in those hot mineral waters that could cure my condition!

To our unbounded delight, Ursula and I were blessed with day after day of glorious sunshine, clear warm skies, and almost complete solitude. Hour upon hour I would soak, soak, stretch, stretch, and exercise, exercise in those springs. As by a miracle the knee began to mend. The pain diminished. I began to walk again—freely, smoothly, and without discomfort. In fact, so complete was this total restoration that a week later I could actually run.

Thank you, Father! Thank you, Father!

Just two weeks ago I read a remarkable account of Handel, who, in the midst of his career, faced a similar dilemma. Somehow he lost his mobility as well as his zest for life—even his capacity to compose great music.

Then he went to a spa at Aachen where day after day he soaked and soaked his weary bones. Suddenly one day he realized that he was being restored. In his ecstasy, he went to a nearby church and began to play the most magnificent music on its great organ. Listeners were astonished! Not long after that, Handel composed the *Messiah*.

They that wait upon the Lord shall renew their strength.

Chapter Two

Challenge of the Classes

In the preceding chapter I mentioned that during the fall season I had been conducting regular Bible studies in a town fifty miles north of our home. On the surface, this may seem a very mundane and ordinary Christian activity, but for me it was not, nor has it ever been, since the first day Christ called me to do this specific service.

For me, it is not a ritual or a rote activity. Unlike many teachers, I have had neither human instruction nor seminary training in the Scriptures. For some thirty-five years I have searched God's Word with unrelenting enthusiasm. It is the Spirit of Christ who has been my Counselor and Instructor.

The truths revealed by Him have become much more practical, workable, and relevant to actual life with Christ than mere theory, theology, or dry doctrine. God's Word, as Christ Himself declared, has become to me spirit and life—His Spirit and His life made real in my personal, intimate, daily relationship with Him, so that, in essence, for me to live is to actually know and share in the life of the Living Christ.

The end result is that when there comes a chance to teach classes in any church, the challenge for me is not merely to disseminate doctrine or information about a historical Jesus but rather to actually introduce Christ in His life and power to the people. I long for people to meet Him in person; to discover the utter credibility of His character; to learn to trust Him in unflinching faith; to then go out with joy to do His bidding and demonstrate their love and unshakable loyalty to Him; thus drawing others to Him.

This is a tall order indeed.

Many who come to the classes recoil from the encounter. They would prefer an academic dialogue on doctrine.

But I am not there to offer academic dialogue. I will not be drawn off into philosophical debates with intellectual dilettantes. If they do not come in order to meet and know Christ in the majestic power of His resurrection life, then it is better that they do not come at all. And, in actual fact, as of old with the scribes and scholars who continually attacked Christ and then turned from Him, the same remains true today—many depart in disgust.

The inviolate truth of God's own self-revelation, inspired and energized by His Holy Spirit, polarizes people. Either they receive His Word of welcome with joy, or they despise and reject Him. Either they are for Him or they are against Him. But to those who receive Him, He becomes their dearest Friend, their closest Confidante.

It is this continuous, ongoing process of watching men and women in the classes accept or reject Christ that is so painful. They are being offered new life, the very life of the Living Christ. Yet so many willfully, stubbornly, selfishly, and blindly choose death—spiritual death and separation from their Savior. He longs to draw them to Himself. Still they scorn His overtures of compassion, love, and passionate concern. They spurn His Spirit!

No wonder He weeps over perishing people.

So do I, in the privacy of my own life.

So do those who pray earnestly for the lost.

It is this pathos that I see so much. It carries great personal pain, for I realize acutely and with great sorrow that I live in a decadent society—in a vain and corrupt culture—among generations in turmoil, tension, and trouble.

Every time I teach a series of studies the scene is more stark.

We cannot delude ourselves about a world so dark.

Except for the inner presence and dynamic power of Christ within I could not triumph against so much trouble.

Because most of my classes are conducted in the form of a discussion, anyone is free to ask questions, to challenge the truth taught, or to make open comment about the subject under study.

This makes for some stormy sessions.

Sometimes the discussion becomes highly charged.

But above all I soon discover those who do not know Christ in living reality. Actually they are seeking truth, and it is an honor and pleasure to introduce them to Christ.

Such occasions are a joyous encouragement from Him. They hearten a man to press on in the face of open opposition. They are a part of Christ's provision to provide the power needed to triumph over trouble in His royal service.

I say this in the utmost sincerity. For with advancing age (I am now in my seventy-fourth year), there is not the same strength of body nor stamina of nerves to always prevail. So the energy to press on, and the enthusiasm to endure hardship and pain and sorrow under Christ's command must come from Him. It is He who is my very life! In company with Him, glorious advances are still made despite all adversity.

Let me here recount some joyous events in order to bring high honor to His name.

That fall it utterly astonished me to see how many hungry hearts turned out for the Tuesday night sessions. The hall in which we assembled was packed with extra chairs. Still the people, all sorts of people, crowded in until they stood around the walls and piled up outside the doors. Surprisingly, there were as many men of all ages as there were women.

A stranger whispered to me, "Phillip they won't be back. We've all heard how tough you are. They will turn away!"

Imagine, if you can, what that does for a man's morale. Talk about trouble on your hands. I had it in truckloads before I ever began the first class.

Quietly, calmly, and in childlike trust I turned to Christ and handed over the entire evening to His supervision. Only He could enable me to triumph in this trouble. I would be acutely sensitive to His Spirit in this tempestuous situation. Many may have come only out of curiosity or contempt or cynicism and would need a tender touch from my Master's hands.

A full hour and one-half later I felt urged to close the class. The people had been so patient, so eager, so attentive to God's Word. My amazement seemed to startle them. Some pled with me to keep on into the night. It was but the beginning.

Despite the stranger's dire prediction; regardless of weather, sports events, or political rallies; week after week, people poured in. And, in the process, lives were changed, men and women came to Christ. I was heartened.

After the series concluded, an eager young couple came to me privately. They were intelligent and alert. They wished to share with me the remarkable impact that the classes had had on their lives. One evening the gracious Spirit of God had come to them with such unusual personal conviction that they could scarcely speak. In awe, silence, and wonder they went home to be utterly alone in the divine presence of Christ.

In the sacred sanctum of their own home, they each bowed before God to surrender themselves completely to His command. In that memorable act of quiet surrender and complete capitulation to Christ, they had discovered the wonder of His grace and joyous pardon. They were a couple set free to follow Him in love.

Their faces reflected the remarkable radiance of the indwelling presence of the Living Christ. He had come now to reside with them and in them exactly as He had promised.

> . . . If a man love me, he will keep my words: and my Father will love him, and we will come unto him, and make our abode with him (John 14:23).

What a remarkable honor bestowed by the Most High upon mortal man! Here in truth, in fact, and in living reality was a demonstration of divine power recreating a couple who had received Him as heaven's royalty. They were in truth being transformed into His children, the recipients of His very life.

Precious moments of this sort made all the challenges of the classes worthwhile. Christ, as of old, was calling out a people for Himself from the crude culture of our contemporary society. So, amid all the pain and pathos of our tragic world it was possible to triumph against the trouble of our times.

A touching note to this story was the unusual way in which they chose to show their personal gratitude to me. The young man, without much comment, handed me a brown bag, roughly wrapped and very cold to the touch. When I got home and unwrapped it with Ursula late that night, we found beautifully prepared kokanee salmon, freshly caught, cleaned, and packed in ice. What a bounty from the hands and hearts of two young people touched by Christ.

Christ the Master of the entire universe had not changed across twenty centuries of horrendous human history. He was still calling men who loved to fish in a lake to follow Him. He was still using the fish from shinning waters to set a feast before His friends. And in that simple way my soul was inspired anew.

Another memorable night, some young men stayed behind after the classes concluded, wishing to speak to me privately. One was obviously what I call a "high rider," decked out from head to toe in a glistening black leather jacket, black leather pants, and black leather boots, all adorned with bright silver studs. His long, coal-black hair was pulled back from his tragic white face in a tight knot. He appeared to be wearing pancake makeup, which only added to the startling austerity of his appearance.

But in his tragic eyes there burned the passion of a soul seeking deliverance from the darkness of despair. Much the same was true for his companion.

He was very blunt with me. "Mr. Keller, I really thought I was a Christian, but when I pray, nothing happens. God does not answer me. Why?" His pal grunted his approval and mumbled that the same was true for him as well.

My reply was equally brief, blunt, and to the point. "I am not a man to pry into your past. Christ already knows about you and every detail of your life. But I must tell you that there is some iniquity in your behavior that stands between you and Him, so He will not hear your prayers." I then quoted Isaiah 59:1–2:

> Behold, the LORD's hand is not shortened, that it cannot save; neither his ear heavy, that it cannot hear: But your iniquities have separated between you and your God,

> and your sins have hid his face from you, that he will not hear.

The young man's tragic eyes opened wide. His jaw dropped and the hot burning words tumbled from his tongue. "It is my hard rock music. I love it!"

Gently, tenderly, and firmly I explained to the two young fellows the dreadful history of hard rock. It startled them to hear that I, as a boy, had listened to this dark sound roll through African nights, long before they were ever born.

When I explained that it was the incomplete rhythm, the syncopated "broken beat," that broke people down, they were shocked and stunned.

"That's it! That's it!" they asserted vehemently, one of them bursting uncontrollably into the typical contortions and gyrations made famous by Elvis Presley. "It's the beat! It's the beat that breaks you up."

I looked at the two young men with enormous compassion and profound pathos. I stood in silence, waiting for Christ's Spirit to prompt me as to what to say next.

Then I spoke softly, earnestly. "The Christian leaders of the growing church in Russia have sent an open letter to the churches of Canada and the United States. One sentence stands out: "Do not send us your evangelists with a Bible under one arm, and your hard rock music under the other arm. This mad music will destroy our youth!"

It was enough!

There was no need to say any more.

I entreated our Father to give them the courage to put things right in their lives. Then I left the empty sanctuary. I did not get home until very late that night.

Surely, surely, with Christ's help these young men could triumph over this great trouble.

A few days later a brief letter came from that church. It bore a remarkable report. The young man who had been all decked out in black called the youth pastor to come over to his home. Together they had loaded all of his sound "stuff"—his records, his tapes, and his CDs into a truck. The total street value amounted to several thousand dollars. Then, in an act of great courage and quiet faith they hauled it away to the city dump.

It was an action that stirred me deeply.

The Living Christ walks and moves among us today. Our part is to permit Him to have His way. Without Him, we can do nothing eternal.

He triumphs against all trouble!

Chapter Three

Taking Out Trees

All my life's experiences have been intertwined with trees—all sorts of trees. In part, this devotion and attraction to trees came from my dad. He went to East Africa as a Christian layworker early in the twentieth century. It was gripped then, as it still is periodically, in the appalling pangs of drought, famine, death, and disease.

The very first duty given to him was to use relief supplies to feed thousands upon thousands of starving Africans. The same sort of scene that has been shown to us so vividly on our TV screens; the same suffering we are familiar with from Somalia, the Sudan, Ethiopia, and Mozambique ravaged the land then.

It was in that furnace of affliction that Dad soon came to have such a remarkable compassion for his African associates. His love, understanding, and deep respect for them became a byword in the country. To thousands and thousands of these perishing people he was much more than an agent from afar handing out relief. He had become a father—"a dada" who loved them with deep devotion and genuine grace.

In his remarkable manner, Dad was at least fifty years ahead of his time. He had been endowed with spiritual perception and practical foresight far beyond his peers. He could see clearly that the Africans with their destructive slash-and-burn technique of clearing land were ravaging their own environment and could save and sustain it only by planting trees by the thousands across the bare hills that were being clear-cut of all forest growth.

Dad sent all over the continent for seedlings from scores of different trees. He would test plant these around our home to see which species survived best under our tough equatorial conditions. As a small lad, tree planting was a large part of my life, and our home became beautiful with trees.

Dad planted hundreds of different eucalyptus, silver oak, and casharina varieties. Some were simply for fuel and firewood. Others were for saw logs that could be cut into lumber for tables, benches, beds, and buildings. Still others were for fruit that could help nourish and sustain the poor people. I once counted twenty-seven different kinds of fruit trees flourishing on our grounds, which had once been but a barren, sun-blasted, rocky hill.

Dad knew deep within his sincere spirit that if the Africans were to regain their self-respect, their dignity, and their honor as God's people, they could not remain paupers. Trees could help heal their land, give shade from the ferocious sun, suckle the water springs again, supply fuel for their home fires, provide timber for their trades, and nourish their families with fresh fruit.

Planting trees was all part of accomplishing God's great, good work in the world of famine and drought. Dad did it with a flourish and with remarkable success. Thousands upon thousands of forest groves sprang up all across the country. The resurgence of new, fresh life on the land was nearly as remarkable as the spiritual renewal and incredible growth of the indigenous churches that flourished under Dad's care. For Dad it was all wonderful to behold.

So, it can be understood why for me this planting of trees became a contagious joy that has never left. It has been an important part of my life.

On the very first ranch I ever owned, I set out more than fifteen hundred sturdy Douglas firs to serve as a giant windbreak against the eternal gales off the sea. I have planted scores and scores of shade trees, fruit trees, and ornamental trees wherever I have lived. To this day, I still love to bring home some wild, forlorn, tough tree from the mountains and give it a second chance to thrive.

Thus, for me to cut down a tree is almost akin to taking the life of a friend. Like the Orientals, I have come to hold trees in great respect and fond affection. Trees, too, are gracious living organisms that contribute so much to the beauty and bounty of the earth. Whenever I must take one out, in sincerity, I do beg its pardon for having to end its life so abruptly.

Unfortunately and unhappily there are occasions on which the wrong trees have been allowed to grow in the wrong place for the wrong purpose. I sometimes refer to these as weed trees, for they are not serving the appropriate use for which they were intended. Then there is little choice but to remove them.

When we came to our present home to live, the surroundings and landscaping pleased us very much. The yard was adorned with a fine variety of trees and shrubs that did much to enhance the location. There was really only one group of trees that posed a serious problem, and, that in the future, I knew would spell real trouble for us.

Unwittingly, a previous owner had planted a number of ragged Chinese elms along the boundary between our house and the neighbor's place. As sometimes happens, the trees were inadvertently established on the neighbor's property, so when later a fence was erected, they were out of bounds.

Chinese elms are notoriously tough, hardy trees. They can survive the hottest summers without water because they have a massive, aggressive root system that searches out and sucks every drop of moisture from the parched soil. They grow at a tremendous rate under the most adverse conditions. Six, seven, eight feet of new growth in a single season is common. They fling their wild and tangled limbs into the sky with abandon, which attracts hordes of insects as well as disease that decimates the leaves.

The end result is a huge, ragged, ungainly growth not always pleasing in appearance and almost impossible to control except at great cost. The limbs simply have to be cut back with cruel severity every spring—a major job for anyone—involving great labor and expense.

When we moved in, it was obvious that the previous owners had tried to prune in a halfhearted way. But because the trees were across the fence the results were repulsive. The trees were misshapen. They were now growing large enough to block out the glorious view of the mountains beyond, but more than that they spelled big trouble for us.

Chinese elms shed millions of tiny, paper-thin seeds. These have an incredible capacity to germinate, take root, and grow wherever they blow. Hundreds upon hundreds began to sprout all over our yard—a truly major task to try to control. Beyond that, every fall, hosts of half-dead, half-brown, half-eaten leaves would fall in clouds over our rockeries, our lawns, and our paths, making for endless extra labor.

For me, as an older person, the elms were trouble. How does one deal with such a dilemma?

It was one of those knotty, tangled problems that has no easy, simple solution. But we decided, trees or no trees, we would and could cultivate a cordial relationship with our neighbor. The trees must not alienate us! We would trust God in our trouble!

One afternoon the neighbor lady came over for a cup of tea. Sitting quietly at the table she suddenly seemed "to see" the trees and how they were blocking our entire mountain view. To my surprise she volunteered that they should be cut back. So I offered to get a friend, skilled in tree pruning, to come over and do the job. We agreed to split the costs, even though they were her trees. Ursula and I even offered to help lug the limbs and load the truck.

It turned out to be a much bigger job than we had ever imagined. By the end of the task we were all tuckered out, our muscles screamed for relief, and our backs ached for a rest.

Although the neighbor lady had been at home all the time we worked, not once did she come out to where we labored or even offer to pick up a single twig. Still the job was done well and we were glad that at least for one year there would be fewer leaves to rake and fewer seedlings to pull out of the yard.

Almost two years later the trees were larger than ever. They were now becoming absolute giants with huge trunks. Their massive roots had not only ruined their owner's lawn, but were invading our yard as well. I had to take a huge old falling ax and cut them off all along the fence. But these giant elms were not to be deterred. The tough pruning only seemed to challenge them to greater growth.

The property changed hands. The new owner had apparently not even considered the effect of the trees either on their own place or ours. After spending hours and hours raking up huge piles of ragged leaves, they must have decided that it was all too much trouble. For this and other reasons they soon decided to sell.

They slipped away quietly. The trees were not touched. In unrestrained exuberance the Chinese elms grew into a giant mass of tangled limbs that now defied anything I could do to restrain them. In our plight we entreated our Father to send new neighbors who would not only be cordial but who would also care enough to confront the challenge of these tough trees.

All that summer a steady stream of potential buyers looked over the property, but no one wanted to buy. As fall approached, our concern increased over the trees.

Then one day something astonishing occurred. Ursula was walking home from the mailbox when she saw a young man strolling on our lawn. Greeting him, she discovered that he was a prospective buyer of the place next door. He was very friendly but expressed great concern to her about the elms. She in turn told him how much work and trouble the trees were for us.

Then he spoke up clearly. "I come from Hawaii where we have such beautiful trees. I can't stand these ugly trees that look so sick and scrawny!" It was agreed that if in fact he got the financing to buy the house the trees would have to be taken out. It was almost too good to be true!

Some weeks passed and we saw no more of him. Now fall was upon us and it seemed sure that nothing had changed. With advancing years and diminished strength, the prospect of our spending hours in the cold autumn winds gathering up leaves was less than encouraging—especially since I already carried such a heavy workload for a man my age. There were classes to teach, books to write, a massive worldwide correspondence to keep up, the ill and aged to visit, a large yard to maintain, winter wood to get in, plus all those leaves.

I was at work in my study one morning when suddenly I was startled by the angry scream of a chain saw next door. In utter amazement I rushed into the next room, looked out the window, and saw the new neighbor and a friend cutting down the largest elm.

The thought shot through my mind: *That fellow really did mean it when he said he hated those trees!* In a rush of excitement, exuberance, and gratitude I exclaimed out loud, "Thank You Father! Thank You Father!" Bounding up the stairs, I pulled on a warm jacket and gloves to go over and help them take out the trees. Happily, it was one of those late autumn days when the wind had died down, the air was calm and still, and a low sun in a clear sky warmed the world just enough to make heavy outdoor labor pure pleasure. In a matter of moments, I exchanged hearty greetings with my brand-new neighbors, offered to lend a hand, and set to work.

It was quickly apparent that I was working with a couple of very unusual young men. Not only were they very hard workers, but they were also skilled in the use of their tools and equipment. They moved with admirable expertise and quiet efficiency. In short order the trees were down on the ground ready to be turned into winter firewood.

Above and beyond all of this remarkable change in our outlook was the gracious, genial manner in which these two men worked together. There was a special sense of mutual esteem and wholesome respect that came as a great consolation to me. Surely, surely our Father had brought about a marvelous solution to our troubles in His own proper time and in His own profound way. It was all beyond our fondest hopes or highest expectations. The simple, categorical statement that God can do exceedingly abundantly above all that we ask (Eph. 3:20) had been demonstrated to us in plain, homespun reality on this fall day.

Ursula, in her happy, hearty way invited us all in for a generous lunch that she had prepared with love and gratitude. In a single day we had not only regained all of our glorious mountain view but also the new friendship of some unusual young neighbors.

After lunch I went out to help clear away some of the limbs and debris that had fallen across the fence. In doing so I made a misstep on the edge of the juniper-covered rock wall. The next instant I lay crumpled on the boulders below with a badly injured body.

Chapter Four

Disabled Again

When I tumbled over the wall, it was obvious that serious damage had been done to my lower spine and pelvic region. Bravely, I staggered to my feet and tried to carry on with the work at hand. But the injuries were deep and damaging. There was little more heavy work that I could do. I knew little then just how long it would take to recover from this injury.

As is my custom in such circumstances, I took a warm bath to help relax the injured joints and muscles. But when I rose the next morning I felt like only half a man. My body was seriously disabled, and at my advanced age any recovery would be long, slow, and very painful. I was up against real trouble—the sort that does not just go away with wishful thinking.

Not to be dismayed by this serious setback, I sought strength of soul and inspiration of spirit from Christ Himself. He was here, present to sustain and support my flagging energy and to quicken my resolve to push on.

But first there were some things moving on my behalf. Quietly I ran them over in my mind and gave Him hearty thanks. We were now into early November and most of the heavy yard work was over for the year—no more lawns to mow, no more long hoses to haul around, no more temperamental sprinklers to move every few hours, no more trees to trim, no more leaves to rake up, and no more winter wood to haul and stack. Much of the heavy physical work was done.

There was time to relax.

There was time to rest.

There was time to reflect.

The Bible studies, too, were almost over. That meant that the long drive back and forth would only need to be made a couple more times. But was I up to this challenge? At least I would give it a shot.

That first trip to the Bible study lingers on as a very bad dream. It was sheer agony to even climb into the car. Somehow the seats no longer seemed suited to my lanky frame. Trying to even get comfortable was terrible torture. My back and hips screamed for relief. I tried assorted cushions and soft, folded wool blankets to diminish the suffering, yet nothing really seemed to help.

Driving under such adversity really was dangerous. Every few miles I would pull off to the side of the road just to rest. I struggled to shift my painful position from one point of torment to another. There was no relief. I even tried driving with alternate legs—not easy in a car with a clutch. So it was that I struggled back and forth to that study session.

The reader may well ask: Why? Why bother? Why not just cancel the classes?

The answers are quite simple: It was my duty to be there because we were dealing with eternal issues and I was convinced that my Father would enable me to triumph against trouble as I trusted Him.

The very next, and last, week a kind and gracious neighbor offered to drive me all the way up and back. In that way the Bible studies were carried through to full completion. And, in His faithfulness to all of us, Christ truly touched many lives among the hundreds who attended.

The reader may also ask: Why did you not see a doctor?

Again the reply is straightforward: I choose calmly to trust God instead because for some forty years He has restored my strength. Christ, my Friend, is also my physician.

It would take time and patience for me to be renewed.

But in a long life of adventures with Him, His healing hands had always restored my life. I could wait for Him in calm confidence!

In all these adversities there was another factor at work that complicated circumstances for us. Namely, we had to make some hard decisions about the winter. Would we now just stay in the north, quietly incarcerated by snow, ice, and howling winds? Or would we be bold enough to break free and spend the winter months in our beloved second home in Santa Barbara where the mountains meet the sea?

I call it our second home not because we have a house there but because our hearts are often there. For many years we made this California community our true home on various occasions. I had taught hundreds of Bible studies in that seaside city with its glorious setting and marvelous climate. We had held classes in homes, in country clubs, in churches—wherever a door was opened to God's Word. And in those diverse places God's gracious Spirit had in fact touched many lives with His transforming power.

I call it our second home because it has an ideal environment in which to write. It is a remarkable location for creative work. With its glorious ambiance amid so much natural beauty and serenity by the sea I had written at least a dozen of my best books.

I call it our second home because there our Father has given us such dear friends. They are precious people who have enriched our lives beyond measure with their gentle kindness, their happy goodwill, and their love that is shown in the profound affection of quiet acceptance.

I call it our second home because in that community we poured our lives, our work, our time, our tears, our means, our prayers, and our compassion into struggling churches and our beloved rescue mission. We invested ourselves there freely, and we loved to keep in touch to see what Christ was accomplishing.

Finally, I call it our second home because there under its balmy climate and along its wind-kissed beaches my health had once been restored. Why could it not happen again?

The previous winter we had fully intended to go south, but it never happened. Every time we were ready to leave, someone, somewhere would call to ask me to take some services, to teach some classes, or to carry out some assignment for the Master. So we never did get away. We deem our service to Him as always more important than our personal preferences. The upshot was that we had not gone to Santa Barbara for two years. Would it happen this winter?

My physical condition now called for us to make some sort of drastic decision. Should I remain quietly at home, counting on rest and relaxation to restore me, or should I accept the challenge and tackle a very tough trip south? Little did we dream how much trouble such travel would cause.

After careful deliberation, quiet discussions, and earnest prayer in seeking our Father's will we decided to go no matter what the consequences.

It is at times like this that God's child must be sure beyond any questioning that it is in fact the Father's wishes that are being carried out and not our own, for if hardships, reverses, or trouble follow, all sorts of doubts and despair can intrude into life. It is very easy for Christians to exult in God's goodness when things go well. But there appear to be great, dark doubts that arise when things go wrong.

It is obvious, then, that certain profound principles must be applied in making long-range decisions according to God's will and intentions for us. Several of them are well known.

1. Our choice should not contravene His clear commands.
2. His interests and His work were to come first.
3. The decision should never dishonor Him or ourselves.
4. If possible, the decision should benefit others as well.
5. There should be an element of divine wisdom in what we choose.
6. If made for purely selfish purposes, the decision is in doubt.
7. The final decision should be accompanied by inner peace and the calm assurance of complying with our Father's will.

It is all very well to put these guidelines on paper. The difficulty comes in applying them in a practical manner that is honest, sincere, and free of pretense. Most of us who earnestly endeavor to walk with our Father in humble and intimate communion know how to read His Word with respect. We also know how to seek the guidance of His gracious Spirit. We learn to trust Christ with implicit confidence for our care. What we seem to lack is a clear understanding of how to proceed in choosing His will in difficult decisions. All of us face occasions when the circumstances of life or the people with whom we are associated, utterly baffle us. We are put under pressure to act, to decide, to do something. But what? What is best? What would give Christ a chance to intervene in our affairs. Allow me to be as helpful as possible here, for this was the deep dilemma before us—to go or not to go? When? How? Where? Why?

First, we must be prepared to wait. This principle was made very plain in the first chapter of this book.

Second, in utter stillness and solitude we need to quiet our souls and calm our spirits, expecting to meet with Christ, prepared to have Him speak to us through His Word.

Third, what His gentle Spirit reveals to us we must be ready to carry out in calm compliance without complaining—even at high personal cost.

Fourth, it is imperative to disengage ourselves, our personal preferences, our pride, and our pleasure from the circumstances or the people who press in upon us. In short, we must detach and set aside our emotions from the decision.

The reader may very well recoil in surprise and shock from what I have just said. But it is an integral part of walking in harmony with our Father, in making decisions in accordance with His wishes, and in trusting Him quietly to triumph against any trouble.

Let me explain further. The human soul is composed of three marvelous capacities:

- the *mind*—to think, reason, understand, and learn
- the *emotions*—to feel, react, entertain attitudes, and act
- the *will* (called "the heart" in God's Word)—to make definite, long-lasting choices and decisions

In most of our day-to-day experiences we live temperamental lives, conditioned for the greater part by our own emotional responses to circumstances and people around us. It is what we see or sense or feel that in a large part determines what we say or do. We are creatures who constantly change because of our fluctuating responses and reactions to the world around us. This is what our Father calls living by sight and not by faith.

So powerful and so pervasive are our emotions that, unless we have become highly disciplined in our minds, our thought processes can be overwhelmed, canceled, led out, and bypassed by our emotional responses. Basic knowledge, hard facts, common sense, or even wisdom itself can all be ignored in the heat and excitement of highly charged emotions.

The tragic end result is that if our emotions are not controlled by Christ; if they are not subject to His Spirit; if they are not governed by God our Father, they will override our wills and make it impossible to choose, decide, or even act. In short, our emotions short-circuit our wills; thus, it follows that we cannot do God's will. We cannot do His bidding. We are unable to trust Him in simple calm faith. Yet, He tells us as His people that we are to live by faith in Him (even in decision making), not by sight.

Perhaps a practical illustration will help clarify this point.

A young lady in a large city loves to walk in the park after work. But she is aware of the dangers of doing so alone. She decides calmly in her mind what steps she should take in case of an attack—run, scream for help, or lash out with full force against her assailant.

It is a lovely summer night and she is strolling alone, lost in the beauty of the setting sun. Suddenly, she hears heavy footsteps behind her. Her pulse quickens. She walks faster. Her emotions take over. She is paralyzed with fear. She cannot run. She cannot scream. She cannot fight. Everything she rehearsed in her mind has been bypassed by her emotions. Even her will is shut down, unable to act. And in those awful moments she becomes a victim.

Later in court, when her assailant is brought before the judge, she must admit that she did nothing to defend herself. She may even be charged with complicity in the crime. That is how subtle and how serious it can be to rely only on emotions in our decisions, which explains our need to disengage our emotions not only in the important choices we make but also in our daily decisions as we seek God's will. When trouble comes, we need to be absolutely sure that it is not of our own choosing.

Our Father honors the person who, with a clear, calm mind and a pure heart (will), in accordance with His own commands, does His will. That individual can live before God and man without fear and without foreboding. Their calm confidence is in Christ. No matter what trouble comes, he or she can triumph against it because all things are made to work out for good by God.

It was in this calm, solid assurance that we decided under our Father's direction to go south. There would be trouble and more trouble. But in that trouble we would see Him triumph.

Chapter Five

Trip to Nowhere

Having made the hard decision to travel to Santa Barbara, we carefully set a definite date in late November. We hoped earnestly that it would still be early enough in the season to miss most of the heavy snowfalls in the high country we had to traverse.

As is my custom, I took the car to the dealer for an oil change and tune-up before leaving on such a long trip. When I took the Hyundai Sonata in, it ran smoothly and silently. When I drove it the eight miles home from town, it began to thunder and roar like a gravel truck. Oh no! Not just now when we were at the point of leaving.

The verdict was that the main exhaust system had burned out. So now the additional cost of preparing the car for the road would burn another $375 hole in my pocket. This was to be a single, sinister omen of what lay ahead of us. In her practical, forthright manner Ursula searched my face for assurance, asking, "Darling, are you absolutely sure we should go?"

It was a legitimate question. At the best of times, she was not overly enthusiastic about the long drives from Canada to California. This time my crippled condition made the prospect even more painful. Now this sudden unexpected expense dampened her spirits more than ever.

I looked at her long and lovingly. She was a brave lady. We have been through many tough times together. When the chips were down she was always game to go. Quietly my reply came out, "Honey, we have determined to do God's will. Only He knows what lies ahead. We will just trust Him. We'll bite the bullet and see this thing through."

Without debate or dispute, she went ahead, packing for the trip. She had a strong premonition that we would need extra bedding, extra towels, extra dishes, extra cutlery, and extra pots and pans to get through the winter. Our plans were to rent a place for several months, and often they were not well furnished.

For my part, I had special plans to write another book during the quiet winter interlude. Several subjects had been suggested to me. So, I packed boxes with all the equipment necessary for this project. The end result was that as the moving day approached we had a veritable mountain of material to load in the car and haul with us. Our only consolation was that a heavily loaded vehicle holds the highway much better under snow-and-ice conditions. Swiftly that thought came to comfort us on the eve of our departure.

We were up well before dawn the next day. With great care and skill from long years of travel we packed the beloved Sonata to capacity. The vehicle hunkered down on the road surface like a sprinter ready to launch from starting blocks. Even loaded to the limit, this remarkable car could fly down the highway with astonishing ease. Driving with such power and response was pure pleasure at most times.

This trip would be different.

This trip would be torture.

This trip would be a test of grim endurance.

Quietly, we bowed our spirits before Christ our loving Lord. We placed ourselves, the car, and the entire expedition in His wondrous care. A bit like Abraham of old, who at the astonishing age of seventy-five set out for the new land to which God called him, was I, approaching my seventy-fourth year and leaving for a place prepared by my Father but still unknown to me.

We had made no definite arrangements as to where we would stay. When pressed, I could only reply in all honesty, "We really do not know where we will stay. I am sure our Father has prepared a place for us. He will lead us to it!"

This was not an act of bravado, nor was it folly. It was my simple step of calm confidence in Christ.

We eased out of our driveway into the early morning darkness. The car handled very well on the road. Fortunately, I had been able to balance the load so the car clung to the road like a crab.

Twenty minutes from our front door I was suddenly driving on the most dangerous of all surfaces—black ice. The road was as slick, smooth, and sinister as newly polished skating ice.

The Sonata, so low slung, so heavily loaded to capacity, so sturdy in its stance, responded nobly to my touch. It did not sideslip or stray on the shiny surface. Instead it held steadily on course as I drove with all the skill and expertise that I had learned in well over fifty years of winter driving.

I had not whispered a word about the ice, but Ursula soon detected in the darkness that we were not soaring down the highway at our usual speed. "Are we on black ice?" she asked rather bleakly, deep concern etched in every syllable.

"Yes," I replied softly, not to alarm her. "This is a slow start to a long, long adventure. Our only hope is that the sun will soon come up and melt it off the highway." My remarks were hardly reassuring. Out loud I then entreated our Father to protect us from this dire danger, beseeching Him for unusual skill as well as some early respite along the road.

To my unbounded joy the black ice suddenly came to an end. Because of unusual weather conditions during the night, it had only covered a stretch of about twenty miles. By the time the sun had risen above the eastern skyline we were soaring south down the road under blue skies and bone-dry pavement.

We stopped to have a drink of hot tea from our thermos, to munch on a hearty homemade sandwich, and to give our Father thanks.

But, oh my bones! My screaming back! My injured hips!

I could hardly climb out of the car.

It was terribly hard to pry myself out of the seat.

And when I did, I could scarcely stand.

In her compassion and concern Ursula asked, "Are you sure you want to carry on all the way to California?" It was a legitimate question, since well over twelve hundred miles of travel still lay ahead of us.

Again I declared my determination to press on. We had made the original choice on the basis of clear guidance from above. It was not that we were indulging our own desires or even deciding "to do our own thing." There was some profound purpose in all this pain. It might take a long time to discover what it was. But our Father was faithful, so I set my face like flint to meet the challenge.

I rearranged the cushions on my seat, changed the angle of the back support, and altered the distance I had to extend my legs to the driving pedals. This would be a long, long day of agony.

Despite the pain, there really was a glorious, golden sheen to this difficult day. The entire drive down through eastern Washington and Oregon, along the winding rivers, across the sagebrush benches, and over the high passes was serene under late-fall sunshine. The highways were perfect, free of any trace of ice or snow.

Ursula and I raised our voices to give thanks again and again. It was almost like driving in a dream world. That late in the season there was virtually no tourist traffic. Even big trucks were few and far between. There was little to impede the Sonata from soaring smoothly on its way south.

At dusk, we gratefully pulled into a familiar motel and settled in for the night. A hot bath helped ease my aching bones.

At 4:00 A.M. we were ready for the road again. Encouraged by the progress we had made the day before, there was a profound inner conviction that this day, despite all my agony, could be another day to triumph against trouble. With energy and endurance from Christ Himself, we could get well down into central California. When I went out to the car, I was aghast. There it stood, sheathed in ice! Even the doors were difficult to open. If the car was like this, imagine what a death trap the highway would be. Gingerly I scraped the ice and frost from the windshield, windows, and mirrors. The sweet-running motor would soon warm up the interior.

We eased our way out onto the dark road, not knowing what treacherous travel lay ahead of us. I calmly entreated our Father to care for us throughout this difficult journey.

Just as with the morning before, the slippery surface came to an end within a few miles. We were crossing the high country just north of Klamath Falls when dense, almost impenetrable fog settled in. My eyes peered into the swirling whiteness, searching for the highway lines to guide us through the gloom.

It was hardly a good start to the long, arduous run that would take us over the high foothills of Mount Shasta and then down into the Sacramento Valley. My earnest prayer was that we would not have to cope with the terrible "tulle fog" that so often enfolds that region.

Every half hour or so I would have to pull off the road. My pain was so intolerable that I had to stretch my limbs, my joints, and my back. The cushion on my seat was arranged and rearranged a score of times during this dreadful drive. Then, finally, I found that by twisting over on my right side and driving with my left leg there was some relief.

At last, at long last, the southern sun dispersed the fog. There were brief interludes of blue sky intermingled with the low-lying clouds. Both of us shouted happily like joyous children, "California, here we come!"

I gave the Sonata her head, and it was like that magnificent car took wing and headed south. Even skeins of wild geese and migrating cranes flying over the great rice fields could not keep pace with us. It was pure pleasure to be traveling under open skies instead of groping our way through dangerous fog.

In swift succession we swept past the valley towns and as the afternoon wore on, through Sacramento and Stockton. "What a blessing," I whispered to Ursula, "that we aren't trapped in heavy traffic here, fighting fog."

At dusk, right on schedule, we pulled into a little crossroads community where we had slept several times during our travels. We went to our favorite hotel requesting the quietest room they could provide for the night.

It was not to be. Both of us were now entirely exhausted from two days of travel in which we had covered a thousand miles. Within an hour of our falling asleep, a wild drinking party started next door. Despite our requests to the front desk for some relief, the racket did not relent until late. Sleep almost eluded us altogether. To my surprise, when I went to check out at dawn the desk clerk offered to refund most of our money.

By now we were a couple of very weary "seniors." Still we pushed on with the expectation that a Christian agent, who had offered to assist us in finding a suitable spot that winter would be eager to help in our dilemma. To our utter astonishment she acted totally indifferent to our needs. Even though she had been alerted to our coming, and we had now traveled twelve hundred miles to reach her office, she could not be bothered to meet us. It was like a last straw for two, tired old people. Put mildly, we were perplexed!

In truth it was like a trip to nowhere.

Where would we go now?

Which way would we turn?

Had we missed our Father's guidance somewhere?

These are common questions that come quickly in a crisis. But they also come, prompted by His gracious Spirit, if and when we pursue our own path persistently.

Perhaps that was our problem at this point.

In the back of our minds we had both entertained the idea that it would be better for us to spend the winter along the coast, somewhat north of Santa Barbara. We hoped to avoid the increasing congestion of that city, its very high cost of living, and the rather hectic, fast lifestyle so typical of Southern California.

In particular, I seemed to be sure that what was most important was to simply find some peace and quiet away from the constant demands of those around me. This seemed to be a legitimate desire for one who was as weary and worn out as I was.

The trouble was that I did not have any inkling of the dark and difficult days immediately ahead of us. Looking back, it is obvious why our Father saw fit to rearrange our affairs—preventing us from making decisions that could have had drastic consequences. He is so trustworthy in taking care of us when things turn out to be the opposite to our most optimistic hopes and appear to take us into trouble. As His child I have come to know that He uses every circumstance, every person in my life for His own best purposes and my best interests. His name be honored!

As a last-gasp measure that horrible day, I suggested to Ursula that we drive up to San Simeon and find a spot to rest. The rhythmic roar of the breakers on the beach, the fragrance of the air off the open ocean, and the compelling cry of the gulls in the wind could begin to mend my battered body.

Chapter Six

San Simeon by the Sea

The late afternoon sun sent its long golden rays across the coastal foothills of the range we had just traversed. This glorious countryside with its rolling rangeland running down to the sea's edge is some of the most exquisite in all the world. It lay there serene and still under the warm glow of the southern sun. Little wonder that California is called the Golden State.

We could already detect the pungent aroma of the air off the ocean. It was a familiar, fresh, sweet fragrance that stirred me deeply. How often across the years and across the miles had I sought the sea's edge for solitude, for stimulation, and for healing. How many hundreds and hundreds of times had I strolled along the shore trusting my Father to restore my spirit, to renew my soul, and to rejuvenate my body.

Always He had been so gracious to do this loving work in wondrous ways. I had written much about this in my books *Ocean Glory, Sea Edge,* and *Wonder O' the Wind*. What He had done before in my younger years, I was now equally confident He could do in my advanced years.

We pulled into the tiny hamlet of San Simeon where a row of motels stood guard above the beach. Across the road was a modest group of condominiums occupied by local people. It was a quiet, gentle sort of spot. We had spent a memorable night there some twenty years before. So we ardently hoped that the same hostelry would welcome us in again.

As soon as we saw the name, The Sands, we knew we were there. It was a lovely name. I asked Ursula to go in and see what was available, while I took a few minutes to stretch my legs, exercise my aching joints, and thus find relief for my burning back.

Soon she returned—all smiles—with that winsome warm glow to her cheeks and eyes that spelled success. She had cast herself upon the mercy of the proprietor, telling him of our tough trip, of our great weariness, and of our sentimental attachment to this spot from so long ago. In cordial response he had compassion on her.

When I went into the office, I was met by a huge man who would have seemed more at home as a giant logger in the northern woods. From within his great frame exuded a gentle spirit. Calmly he told us that he would give us an ocean-side room with a view of the beach for roughly half the usual charge. But this generous offer was only good for a few short days. Then it would be Thanksgiving and room rates would more than double. And more seriously, there simply were no vacancies.

We walked into the spacious, inviting room and drew back the drapes. There before us the breakers burst in white foam on the sands. We hugged each other hard. We were back, and we were humbly grateful for this simple shelter for the next few days. It was to be a quiet interlude that we so desperately needed. In deep gratitude we whispered softly, "Thank you, Father. Thank you, Father."

Swiftly and smoothly Cheri (Ursula) began to unpack the few things needed to make the room more like a home. She has a deft touch, arranging articles around us in such a way that one is quickly comfortable and at ease. In a matter of minutes a convenient pot of water was boiling so she could serve a piping hot cup of tea with some of her beloved cookies that she had packed away in a secret spot.

Refreshed and contented, she said to me, "Darling why, don't you go out and take a tramp on the beach? It will do you good." How well she knows exactly what I need. Within moments I had slipped into rough pants and shoes. The sands beckoned, and I was off.

The western sun was sinking steadily, but still there was time for a tramp. I sat down on a driftwood log, pulled off my socks and shoes, hid them among some rocks, rolled up my pants to my knees, unbuttoned my shirt to the wind, and began to walk barefoot in the sand.

"You are home!"

"You are home!"

It was a simple refrain beating deep within.

The soft cool sand between my toes was like a tonic. The surge of the sea around my ankles, my calves, and my legs brought a serene sense of well-being to my body. I dashed handfuls of the strong salt water over my arms, over my face, and over my aching neck and shoulders. There the droplets cooled my skin and dried slowly in the setting sun.

I wandered on and picked up shells scattered on the sand. I picked up bits of driftwood lodged among the rocks. I picked up pebbles of all sorts that had been polished by the tumbling action of the waves.

"Yes, Father, I am at home!"

Pure joy, pure pleasure, and pure appreciation poured out of my innermost being. I could not staunch the salty tears that trickled down my face to mingle with the salty drops of ocean water that clung to my cheeks.

The reader may scoff, but I am a man who finds enormous delight in simple things. I see them as gracious, generous gifts from my Father's kind hands. So this interlude of stillness, solitude, and serenity on this wave-battered beach was to me a precious prize far beyond my ability to define.

Little did I know or even imagine how much I needed this brief refreshment before the grim weeks that lay ahead. It is fortunate that our Father does not let us see into the future. In His mercy, kindness, and gracious wisdom He invites us instead to simply take His great, strong hand and walk with Him in quiet faith *today*. It is He who helps us over the hard spots. It is He who carries us over the complex problems. It is He who holds us in gentle safekeeping.

> For I the Lord thy God will hold thy right hand, saying unto thee, Fear not; I will help thee (Isa. 41:13).

For years and years I had claimed His commitment to me. Again on that golden evening, on that golden strand of sand, I took Him at His Word once more. He was there! We were walking hand in hand. Come what may, all was well. Little did I know that the next day would turn out to be very tough. It would be a time of trouble. Only His great, good hand holding mine could help me triumph against that trouble.

Because our cozy accommodation at The Sands was available to us only for a few days, Ursula and I felt compelled to get out and search for long-term winter quarters. Little did we anticipate the shock that awaited us.

First off, I went to see an agent who appeared to be very cordial. She arranged for us to meet with her and her husband in short order, but when they discovered that we were people of modest means, they quickly dropped us. One thing that did come through clearly from that encounter was an awareness that it would be almost impossible to rent anything in the area at a reasonable rate.

It was obvious that this somewhat secluded segment of the central California coast had been "discovered" by vacationers from all over the North American continent as well as from Europe. They too were looking for peace, quiet, and some measure of solitude away from the big cities. And they were prepared to pay a high price for privacy in such a pristine setting.

However, we are not the sort of people who are put off easily. If there seems to be a chance of accomplishing a mission, we will pursue every opening that is offered. In this case we decided to divide up the territory between us. Ursula agreed to go from agency to agency in the nearby village of Cambria. This is where most of the rentals would be. I offered to go from place to place along the beaches to see what might turn up. We agreed that we would leave no stone unturned in our search for a suitable spot.

When we met again, both of us had rather grim faces. It was obvious that nothing was available, at least not until well into the next year. We had each been told the same story. Visitors from Chicago, New York, Boston, London, and Berlin, to say nothing of those people from the larger cities of Los Angeles and San Francisco, had booked up all the accommodations long ago.

In our most somber moments, it had never occurred to us that this might be the situation facing us. We almost felt like a couple of waifs, wandering the streets, wondering just what to do or where to go.

To complicate our circumstances even more, I became violently ill the next morning. It was a grim reminder of the terrible sieges of tropical dysentery that I used to endure as a boy. The night before, I had ordered fresh fried clams for my evening meal, so there was also the possibility of having been poisoned by this seafood.

Whatever the cause, Ursula had a very ill man on her hands. In her decisive way, she decided to walk over to a cute little gift shop she had found and ask the proprietor for help. To her unbounded joy she was able to pick up a bottle of Kaopectate and bore it back in triumph. The simple remedy had a remarkable impact on me. By the next day the condition had cleared up enough for me to dare to drive again.

We decided then and there that the time had come to seek our Father's guidance for the next step. Walking with Him in quiet faith calls not only for a childlike trust in His capacity to lead us aright but also the implicit determination to do His bidding day by day in calm confidence—no matter the personal cost. He had made it crystal clear to us at home, before we ever left, that we were to spend this winter in California. We had come this far against incredible difficulties. Where, now, did He wish us to go?

Calmly, softly, without allowing my emotions to enter the discussion, I explained to Ursula that I was convinced that we had to set aside all our own personal desires—our yearning for a secluded spot by the sea, our longing to be away from city noise, congestion, and traffic. Our desire to just be alone to write a book would have to be given over to our Father without debate or dispute. If He had other plans, other purposes, yes even other pain for us, we should be willing to accept His arrangements of our affairs. This is not easy to do. Try it sometime.

One thing was obvious. We were in the wrong part of the

state. Surely, steadily, every opening had been closed in our faces. And I had lived long enough in company with Christ to have learned not to kick in the door and force my way in where He did not want me to go.

Only one alternative remained. We would quietly pack up the car and head southwest to Santa Barbara. It would be Thanksgiving Day in less than forty-eight hours. The prospect of finding any accommodation there was about nil. "I am convinced our Father has a place prepared for us," I spoke with unshakable assurance. "Let us just ask Him to direct us as we drive down today." Ursula did not relish the idea of being on the road again, especially since we had no idea where the trip would end.

Ursula's nesting instinct is very powerful. She is willing to wander with me all over the world. But at the end of the adventure she wants some assurance of a spot to rest and nest. On this morning she urged me to put the pedal to the metal, so to speak, to send the Sonata cruising down the coast at top speed.

As we drove, we said very little.

The California countryside was still, dry, and hot. Its appearance seemed to match our own bareness.

"O Lord I believe, but help my unbelief!" The odds seemed so great against us. No spot to rest, no place to nest! So we sped south like the wind.

But you cannot outpace the wind of God's gracious Spirit. He easily protects us even in our flight and amid our fear. He pursues us down the tangled trails of our troubles. Christ makes a calm commitment to us as His companions.

> . . . I will not fail thee, nor forsake thee (Josh. 1:5).

I clung to that assurance. He was here. Something was sure to open up for us!

Just as we approached the northernmost outskirts of Goleta, a small rural community just northwest of Santa Barbara, a stirring, compelling, and clear inner conviction swept into my spirit: *Try the New Horizons.* This was a retirement community. I had not been there for over fifteen years and had forgotten where to find it.

The instant I mentioned it, Ursula fully agreed.

Almost as if moved by our Master's hand I took the next exit ramp, swung over the roaring freeway, and within two blocks, along an avenue of golden amber trees, saw the shining, golden name plate New Horizons on a sturdy stone wall draped with beautiful bougainvillea.

We drove to the main lodge. Outside there was a glass case with notices inside, among them vacant suites to rent! How faithful you are Father! In joy, we hugged each other!

Chapter Seven

Settling In

Inside the handsome lodge, built in Polynesian style, there was a free phone that we could use. Quickly I called the agent who had several units to rent. Her pleasant reply was not only encouraging but almost electrifying. She would be over to meet us in a matter of minutes.

True to her word, she pulled up to the lodge, stepped out of her car, and greeted us warmly. It was almost as if she had been expecting us. She was a startling contrast to the difficult, arrogant agents we had approached previously.

We were only in her company a few minutes when I received the unshakable conviction that she was serving us as "an angel of the Lord." Her cordial courtesy, her genuine concern to provide us with a suitable suite, and her calm efficiency were remarkable.

She showed us a number of vacant units before we finally decided on one that appeared to be in a suitably private location. It was surrounded by green lawns, an assortment of beautiful pines, golden amber, and olive trees as well as by various flowering shrubs. Ursula was ecstatic about the roses, the poinsettias and the bountiful bougainvillea. It was a glorious garden setting!

The suite itself was unfurnished, but it boasted a beautiful view of the golf course and the beautiful hills beyond. There was a handsome cut-stone fireplace in the front room and in one corner a cute compact kitchen. It boasted two bedrooms, two tiny bathrooms, and endless cupboards. It would do nicely.

Our genial agent was sure that we could take immediate possession if she could find the owner, who was away golfing. She left us in high hopes. While waiting for her return, I seized a broom on the outdoor patio and went to work.

Obviously no one had occupied the place for some time. The outdoor patio was sprinkled with bougainvillea blossoms that had blown off the vines adorning the building. In an act of simple faith I swept them all up, confident that this was the place prepared for us by our loving Father.

The sidewalks, too, needed to be swept. So I set to with a will. Soon they sparkled in the sun. The dry accumulation of fallen pine needles, old pine cones, and brilliant rich leaves off the golden amber trees were swept away. "It's all ready for us to move in," I said as I smiled at Cheri.

In about an hour the agent was back, waving the thumbs-up signal to us. She too was all smiles. She had succeeded. The deal was done, and we could quietly unpack the car, so heavily loaded with all our gear.

Ursula's remarkable feminine intuition that we would need extra bedding, dishes, and even pots and pans had been absolutely correct. In this place there was not even a bed, a table, a cup, or a spoon—nothing!

Our dear agent detected our determination to move in that very hour. So, in her compassion and concern she offered us a table, two chairs, and a lovely lamp from her own home. What a gentle, gracious gesture! She assured us that we could rent some furniture, though it would not be delivered until the next day.

Like a couple of hardy, happy-go-lucky, teenage campers we hauled in all our baggage. It surprised me how much stuff the Sonata had carried for over thirteen hundred miles with such ease. Quickly I arranged a bed on the floor for the first night while Cheri unpacked all her dishes and utensils for the kitchen. We were "in" for the winter, never dreaming of the trouble that we would encounter in this place.

I cannot recall what sort of supper we shared that night, but I suspect it was soup, bread, and cheese, with a cup of tea to warm the cockles of our hearts (an old, old British saying).

Weary with so much uncertainty and physically tired with so much bone-breaking travel, we soaked ourselves in a soothing bath, and then crawled beneath our blankets on the floor. We were home! Deep contentment enfolded us.

Before turning in for the night, I had hiked over to the lodge and called our closest friends in Santa Barbara. They were thunderstruck to hear that we were already settled in at the New Horizons. Completely unknown to us, our friend's head office had been moved out to Goleta. As it turned out, he was directly across the street from our suite, only a stone's throw away. Little did I realize then what a bonus that would be for us in the months to come. Again, our Father had not only prepared a place for us, but He had also arranged for some of our dearest friends to be virtually next door when we needed them most desperately in the dark days that lay ahead.

As I travel gently down the trail in my twilight years I am overwhelmed by the remarkable provisions made for me by my Father. Sometimes it seems that God Himself takes enormous pains to prepare the path that He and I share. But beyond this, there are the people that He brings along that path to share it with me. They are often plain, unpretentious, but very precious people. On this particular night I was again profoundly touched by the amazing arrangements made on our behalf. Our friends insisted that we come over and celebrate Thanksgiving with them. It was wonderful! As I walked to my new home under the southern stars, there welled up within me enormous, powerful, overflowing thanks and gratitude to Christ for all His wondrous care.

Somehow, everything seemed so right and so very satisfying. We were surrounded by the serene assurance that at last we were where we belonged. As of old, we could honestly say,

> . . . I being in the way, the LORD led me to the house of my master's brethren (Gen. 24:27).

With this sweet assurance, a palpable peace pervaded my soul and spirit.

At dawn the next morning I arose, dressed, and slipped outside to take a slow walk around our area. The grounds of New Horizons encompassed some forty acres of choice land on the Goleta flood plain—some of the most fertile soil in all of North America. The soil is six hundred feet deep in some places and on it plants, trees, shrubs, and grass grow and flourish under the benevolence of such a choice climate.

What impressed me most, however, was the meticulous care with which all the grounds were manicured. The whole development reflected the care and loving attention it received from the gardeners. Someone later said to me, "It impresses one as a choice South Pacific paradise." I loved it. It was a pleasure to be amid such exquisite surroundings. We were honored indeed.

Soon after breakfast we left for downtown Santa Barbara to make the necessary arrangements to rent furniture for the winter. Again we met a courteous and helpful young lady who immediately understood our predicament. Swiftly and efficiently, she arranged for a truck to deliver a bed to our new home, though we would have to wait an extra day because of Thanksgiving to get the tables, chairs, couch, and lamps that we needed.

She urged us to rush back to our suite so the bed could be delivered. It was good that we did because we got there just in time. I rejoiced that at least a bed would be better than a hard, cold floor for my aching joints. The bed was but the beginning of many sorrows surrounding our rented furniture. The girl at the office was gracious and helpful indeed, but she had absolutely no control over the quality of the pieces that were delivered from their warehouse sixty miles away.

The truckers were a rough, tough crowd and cared little about the clients. The first bed they brought was a dreadful disaster. It had shattered springs and a torn covering. I really could not help but laugh hilariously at such a horror. Happily, they agreed to exchange it when the next load came.

The next batch of rented furniture turned out to be especially troublesome for Ursula. She has a fragile chest condition and is extremely sensitive to smoke. When the delivery men carried in the couch, it reeked of cigar smoke. The previous renter was without a doubt a "couch potato" of giant proportions who had pretty well wrecked the couch with his massive weight while impregnating all of its fabric with the foul smoke of his cigar. So that piece, too, would have to be replaced.

Just at that juncture we heard a great, shuddering crash on the sidewalk outside. As I stumbled awkwardly to the door, I saw that the two tables we had ordered had fallen off the transfer cart and had gone scraping across the concrete sidewalk on their tops. Both had severe scratches and scars all across them, with their legs all askew at awkward angles like wounded bucks on their backs.

The Hispanic workers never batted an eye. Quickly they pulled soiled hankies out of their pockets, spat on them vigorously, and hurried to try and erase the scratch marks. I did not bat an eye either. Years in Africa, long ago, adjusted me to such tactics. But, with a grin to myself, I knew that this episode dare not be revealed to Ursula. It would just be too much. For three horrendous months she did her best to cover over the scratches and scars that had come with the furniture. Oh what fun! Or was it?

Eventually, after both of us became very ill, and demanded a fresh couch, the furniture people showed up with a different one. They also brought along a proper pedestal lamp that actually gave light, to replace the previous one that never did work. The whole furniture situation was all a bit like pulling teeth. One had to tug and pull to extract anything at all from these difficult suppliers.

One thing that I kept telling Cheri was that we simply could not afford to get angry over such awful service. A hot outburst would not erase the scars or change the couch. It was all part and parcel of learning a bit of patience under adversity and seeing the funny side.

I lost track of how many times furniture came and went from that place. What did not escape my attention was how the truckers thought it was all a great and wonderful joke, so we all laughed together.

Counterbalancing the frustrating furniture situation were two wonderful advantages that this special location gave us. The first advantage was our proximity to the nearby shopping center. It was a fairly modern development that to our surprise provided all the services that we would need throughout the winter—the best part being that, for Ursula, the shopping center was within easy walking distance of our door. She is a sturdy little lady and an excellent walker. Being absolutely free to go to the shops in a matter of minutes meant so much to her. Often she would come back bearing all sorts of "bargains" and "special buys," which she was sure saved her enormous sums of money. She would be smiles—all smiles.

For nearly twenty-five years I have tried to convince this dear little lady that "anything you don't really need is not a bargain—no matter how little you pay." Still, she was sure that she had struck gold. That was the fun—just finding it.

One of her favorite "finds" were the delicious barbecued chickens sold by the supermarkets on certain days of the week. Literally bursting with joy and a hearty appetite, she would bring one home carefully wrapped twice over to keep it piping hot. She would place this golden-brown bird on the scarred table and we would consume it like a pair of hungry wolves, eating it with fresh bread and hot tea. What a banquet! How blessed we were.

The other enormous advantage that came to me in this place was its proximity to a beautiful golden stretch of beach. It took less than ten minutes to get there. Any day that the weather was fine and my frail body was up to a hike along the shore, I was down there early in the morning.

At that hour of the morning scarcely a dozen other people would be on the beach. Perhaps there would be a serious fisherman in search of his supper, but often there was no one but me, the pelicans, cormorants, gulls, curlews, and sandpipers. There was serene solitude.

I would walk for miles if I felt strong. The soft sand beneath the soles of my feet, the swirl of the waves around my legs, the fresh aroma of seaweed on the shore, the warm sun on my face, and the invigorating breezes blowing off the ocean could literally work wonders for me when I so desperately needed their healing touch on my tortured body.

What benefits from my Father!

What beauty all around me!

What pure pleasure just for the taking!

On that strand of shining sand, though, there would be a

struggle to regain my health, my strength, and my energy. I did not see the struggle at first nor could I imagine that it would be so severe later on.

In the meantime, I was delighted to have this world of sea, sky, sun, and sand so close at hand. What a bounty!

Chapter Eight

Thanksgiving

Thanksgiving, because of its inherent simplicity, has always been my favorite festive occasion of the year. It is not encumbered with ancient religious traditions that have been twisted by time. It is not debated and disputed by various segments of society. Apart from the sale of turkeys, cranberry sauce, and sweet potatoes for the hearty meal, it has not been marred by crass commercialism.

The Thanksgiving banquet is a joyous reminder that the early settlers who came to this continent were grateful to God for all His bounties and blessings to them. The season is a gentle moment of grace in which we, amid all of the technical sophistication, need to recall humbly that all that we have and are have come as generous gifts from above.

When Ursula and I assemble with others to celebrate this occasion, our center of attention is focused less on our fun and more on the greatness of our Father who cares for us in such wondrous ways. For me, to even be invited to a friend's home for this occasion is a high honor, for it is a time of great joy and the sincere giving of thanks.

As mentioned in an earlier chapter, our close friends who lived nearby asked us to share their Thanksgiving. This was doubly generous because their own family was also to be there.

There would be a full house, replete with fun, love, and good cheer. It was our very special joy to be there.

We had watched this family mature into a solid group of adults who truly loved and honored God. They were bound together with strong chords of mutual respect, affection, and deep loyalty. Goodwill, generosity, and lighthearted fun flowed freely among them. So it was a profound pleasure to be part of such a genial group. One couple came from Colorado, another from Nevada, the third from California, and we from Canada.

It was a glorious late November day, and the whole earth seemed to be wrapped up in the golden sheen of the southern sun as we drove over. The owner's big handsome cat, all gold and white, met us just outside the front door. Her nostrils twitched with the tantalizing aroma of roasting turkey drifting out the door. She would be celebrating as well!

Inside there were hearty hugs all around, fond embraces with faithful friends, and joyous smiles for those not seen for months and months. Somehow, in the open honesty of our mutual affection and respect, we were all "family." This was a precious moment to be savored.

Among us there was one child. He was the firstborn grandchild and a bit under the weather with some sort of illness common to children. His mother seemed to have picked up the same contagion, so both of them were coughing and choking with chest congestion.

As it turned out, Ursula and I were seated directly across from the child and his mother. The distance between us was not great, and could be easily traversed by any germ or virus bent on taking over new territory. At the time, this thought scarcely entered my mind. But a few days later, flat on my back, it would assume a major role in my memory.

The meal, as with most Thanksgiving dinners, was a masterpiece. It has always aroused my greatest admiration to see how a hostess can prepare such a superb meal out of an ordinary kitchen. Not being a cook, it all spells pure magic to me.

Not only have I been endowed with a hearty appetite all my life, but I have also been endowed with an acute sense of thankfulness for good food, probably in part because as a growing lad there was often not enough to ease my hunger pangs. To this day, abundant meals are a special treat.

The golden turkey, the steaming potatoes smothered in butter, the crimson cranberry sauce, and the heaping bowls of abundant fresh salad were more than enough to rejoice over.

As the evening shadows from the pine trees lengthened across the lawn, a fine fire was started in the open fireplace. We gathered around the flickering flames, quiet and contented, listening to majestic music chosen for the occasion. The day had been an unforgettable occasion—a rare and beautiful gem to be stored in our memory vaults. Another gentle and genuine celebration of the goodness of our Father. As if to say *good night*, the gentle, golden cat came over and climbed softly into my lap. Her purring was telling me, *So glad you could be here—come again soon*. It was a fitting farewell.

Ursula and I then left quietly, giving the family ample time to relish each other for the rest of the evening. We were richer, much richer, than when we came. But, we also bore with us a contagion that would spell trouble.

On the other side of the coin there had burst into my life this day a surprise package wrapped in unusual mystery. Life for me has always been a bit like that. I call these unusual, unexpected events beautiful bonuses from my Father. Often they come at some crucial crisis just when His encouragement and His good cheer give a glorious lift to life.

During the course of our Thanksgiving dinner, the young mother of the sick child had looked at me very earnestly and asked an astonishing question. "Phillip, have you had a chance to see a copy of your latest book?" It seemed such a simple, sincere sort of question.

"Which book do you mean?" I replied with raised eyebrows.

"Oh, it is a copy of a very large volume," she replied calmly and softly. "Actually it is an anthology compiled from a number of your best-selling works. It is a very handsome, beautiful production, but huge!"

At best, all I could do under the circumstances was to express both shock and surprise. When she saw my astonishment the dear lady expressed her deep regret that she had not brought a copy of the work with her. She had come across it in one of the Christian bookstores in Las Vegas where she and her husband live and work.

I did my best to mollify her emotions. Obviously this was a momentous matter in my life. For one thing, an anthology of an author's works are generally compiled only after he is deceased. The thought, fantastic as it seemed, flashed through my mind, *Perhaps they do think the tough old mountain man has kicked off at last.* I had to chuckle to myself at the idea, and in mock derision called back, *Not yet! No, not yet.*

The second mystery was that there had not been a single word of communication, not a solitary letter, and not even one phone call from any of the various publishers engaged in this major production. It all seemed impossible and absurd. I had worked with some of these publishing houses for over thirty years. Surely, they could not be so silent, so secretive, or so insensitive about an author's part in a project of this magnitude.

Of course I kept these concerns to myself. For this was neither the time nor place to trot out the long list of times when there had been trouble with publishers. But I did ask the lady if she could recall who had published the book. She could not, but she had been given a sales catalog of their publications. She promised to send me a copy of it when she got home. My mind was at ease for the moment. Nothing more was said. Let sleeping dogs lie for the present. But this was something big, something mysterious, something baffling.

Having been a serious writer for well nigh fifty years, having worked closely with some seventeen different publishing houses during that time, and having had forty-four books published worldwide in twenty-six languages I thought I had seen it all. Not so.

At times I could only laugh. Surely it is better to laugh than to cry, to give way to anger, or to rant and rave. No, with God's grace I would not allow my emotions to take over in a tirade. Christ's Spirit could control my conduct. He could impart to me the very mind of Christ in order that I might act in dignity. Yes, in time of trouble, Christ could enable me to triumph, not only over the obstacles outside but also over the fierce temper inside my soul that only He could tame.

It was time to turn to other interests and other people. Among these was one of our dearest friends—a widow. When she heard that we were in town, she hurried over to see us.

This sounds easy, but actually her home was high up in the foothills of the Santa Ynez Mountains, at least sixteen miles from us. To reach us she had to drive down the coast and across the city of Santa Barbara to its northwestern suburb of Goleta where we were ensconced.

This drive took a lot of time. Yet, she and her dear family were to do it again and again and again when we became so ill. I never, ever think of her without the clear conviction that she was a chosen servant of the Most High, sent to us in mercy amid our distress.

The simple, compelling statement she often made to me was, "Phillip, it is a deep delight, an honor, a privilege to serve you precious people." If ever there was a lovely lady endowed with Christ's own gracious "servant spirit" it was her.

On her first visit, with the strong, sweet intuition that some women have, she came bringing all sorts of useful household items. They were the sorts of things that would help Ursula in the kitchen, and add comfort to the rest of our living quarters. She had packed extra pots and pans, bowls, plates, tumblers, cutlery, and other cooking utensils in her car. And how grateful and truly joyous Ursula was to see them come. Then she brought extra bedding, spare blankets, and even a warm sleeping bag. At first, we felt almost overwhelmed by it all. It seemed too much. Never did we dream just then how much all of this generous provision would mean in just a few days when we both became so ill.

In her kind, gentle, and gracious way she was sure that we needed every item. So in hearty gratitude we gave our loving thanks, not only to her but also to our loving Father. In His generous concern for us as His children, He had prepared both a place for us as well as precious people who truly cared. I called them all God's angels in disguise.

Chapter Nine

The Great Illness

No doubt the illness would have been less severe if my general health had been more robust. But, by the time we had reached California and had settled in for the winter, my physical stamina was gravely diminished—not only because of the injuries endured during the fall but also because of the high level of emotional stress and spiritual exertions over the entire year.

Early in the spring, my dearest friend had been stricken with cancer and died. His call home was a great gain for him, but I missed his genial presence greatly. Then another friend underwent major heart surgery. In that case, too, there was an acute sense of loss and deep sorrow. Another cheerful comrade suffered a major stroke that bound him to the strict confines of a wheelchair. Of course I do not claim that such incidents are unique to my life alone. They are part and parcel of the pain, grief, and separation of advanced age. At last count Ursula and I have lost some fifty friends in the last few years.

It cannot but leave great gaps in life.

The torn fabric of our friendships is fragile.

The question remains, "Who will be the next?"

I press on. Who knows when my call will come.

Yet the trail one travels is sprinkled with tears while softly the dear familiar faces fade away.

None of this is easy!

In His compassion and tender mercy, our Father does fill some of the gaps with young friends and fresh faces. Nevertheless the constant attrition of older folk brings unusual burdens that are a sorrow for the soul.

It had also been a full year of teaching Bible studies away from home. In all, this work was carried on for twenty weeks. Each session entailed some two full hours of teaching to say nothing of the question-and-answer exchanges at the conclusion. Those Bible studies represent more study, more preparation, more time devoted to prayer and communion with Christ than many ministers give in a year. This outpouring of spiritual life and truth simply means that a man becomes "broken bread" in the Master's hands.

It is no small wonder that Christ Himself often had to slip away from the crowds to find solitude, stillness, and time to be alone with His Father. There may be some public speakers who relish the limelight, but for me it demands enormous self-discipline and self-denial to endure public scrutiny. Still, it is part of His purpose for me as His servant. So I set my course to do His bidding.

Much to my joy, the studies all year were blessed in a most remarkable manner. The Word of the Lord was received with gladness. His gracious Spirit moved upon souls in deep, life-changing conviction. Christ Himself was exalted on high so that our Father was pleased to draw men and women to Him.

For a man so late in the twilight of life this was heartening. Again and again my spirit rose to Christ in praise and gratitude. Nonetheless the great labor had exacted its toll on my strength. Driving one hundred miles back and forth to the classes each time left me weary. Little wonder that I succumbed so severely to a strange malady.

At first I was sure it was malaria again.

The symptoms were very similar—high temperatures, atrocious lassitude, severe aches and pains in joints that already where in agony, loss of appetite, dizziness, almost no energy, severe sweating, steady loss of weight and strength, and the inability to rest.

Life seemed to be coming to a standstill.

Any and every energy was long gone.

Hour after hour I lay inert as a log.

I chose to lie on the couch—even though it reeked of smoke—and stare out the glass doors. There was some solace in the green grass of the golf course that grew right up to the edge of our concrete patio. Beyond that, on the skyline, a gorgeous liquid amber tree and a white-barked birch were adorned in their autumn glory. But little by little their fall foliage was being stripped away by the wind and soon only bare branches would remain.

In my extreme weakness and fatigue I began to wonder to myself if, like the fallen leaves, my life would soon flutter to the ground in a last farewell. I had not been so low in years. Most importantly, I was ready for the last call to come home. My life had been full and overflowing up to this time. All was in order. In childlike helplessness, I quietly waited for my Father to make the next move.

Lying there day after day I found ample time to reflect, to pray, and to meditate quietly over the deep issues of life. I felt no inner anxiety or alarm of any sort. I was completely reconciled to either live or die—die or live. There persisted in my awareness, dull as it was, an absolute unshakable assurance that my Father in His wisdom knew all about my extreme weakness. Despite its debilitating effect on my body some great good would come of it.

He has the most remarkable capacity to bring His light into our darkness. His gentle, gracious love into our despair. His triumphant life into our deadly troubles, serious as they may seem. In short, He can make any calamity, any crisis, any apparent catastrophe serve His purposes and also serve our best interests as well.

Of all this I was sure.

How it would happen I did not know.

But gently and patiently I would wait.

There was really only one great distress. I had not a single thread of ambition left in me to do any work, any writing, any correspondence. Christmas was approaching, but there would be no cards, letters, or greetings going out to friends. Most would think that they had been forgotten.

I had come to California fully intending to write a book, but it was not to be. Not a single sentence would go on the page. In fact, I felt so feeble that I sometimes was convinced that my last work had been done.

At times like this, Christ Himself by His presence and by His own sweet Spirit, draws back the drapes from our world-weary eyes. He permeates the suffering, the stillness of our illness, and the moments of our mourning, and we get a rare glimpse into the essence of life itself.

We see past the pretense and pantomime of human fallibility with incredibly clear perception. We see with vivid intensity how much of what we value is vain, empty, and transient. There is burned onto our conscience the acute, red-hot realization that only what is done in gentle, healing love for others is of enduring worth. The others I refer to here include not just men and women, boys and girls but also God, our Father, God our Friend the Living Christ, God our Fellow Companion and Counselor, the Holy Spirit. And, yes, besides these, all our fellow travelers in time and space—be they trees, grass, flowers, fields, and all our friends of hoof, wing, or paw.

The searching, burning questions come back again and again.

Have I truly, honestly, earnestly lived in love?

Have I laid down my life to help others?

Have I made the earth a better place?

Have my days brought help and healing?

Have others had a glimpse of God in my life?

Have my ways produced goodwill?

Have I made a difference?

A man does not meditate on such themes without serious soul-searching. No doubt they are a prelude to the awesome day when I must stand stripped in the presence of the Most High to render a full report of my behavior on earth.

Then all the playacting will be an affront.

No longer can little white lies and lame excuses do the trick.

Cover ups, double-dealing, and intrigue will be exposed.

All the flimflam of falsehood will go up in fire. What fire? The passionate purity of His presence.

Yes, pain can be a very purifying ordeal.

The furnace of affliction takes care of much trash.

The crucible of suffering sorts out a person's priorities.

There is no place here to play games.

No wonder much of the world's finest art, music, literature, and other inspiration has been produced amidst great pain. It has been shaped amidst deep sorrow and perfected in awesome adversity.

It is always this way.

It must be so in the very nature of things.

Only that which endures is purged and purified by pain.

Are we surprised then that our Father permits it?

Why do we shrink from suffering?

So many pastors and preachers insist that suffering is all of Satan. What a delusion and deception.

Our Father Himself, because He is our Father, He cares, and He arranges our affairs for our utmost and eternal benefit, subjects us to the discipline of suffering to conform us to Christ's own choice character.

As I lay, so feebly, so helplessly, so useless, so inert upon that couch of agony, the reassuring phrases from the gracious Spirit came to me with enormous reassurance. In them I found profound solace for my soul, quickened faith for my spirit, and brave new healing for my body!

Our earthly fathers discipline us, and we treat them with respect, though we eventually die. Shall we not be still more submissive to the Father of our spirits and live?

> It is true that they disciplined us for a few years according as they saw fit; but He does it for our certain good, in order that we may become sharers in His own holy character (Heb. 12:10 Weymouth).

There it is!

There is the answer to all our "whys."

There is the key that unlocks all the problem of pain.

Across the centuries of human history authors from all kinds of backgrounds have written books about the problem of pain. I have read a number of them, not one of which satisfied my searching spirit. All their profound philosophies, their complicated theories, as well as their deep and sometimes devious doctrines did me no great good.

I am an ordinary man on the road of life.

I am a plain person who wants plain answers.

I am not helped by smooth, slick sophists.

If I am one who must suffer, and there has been much, much suffering during my earthly sojourn, then there must be good reasons for it. I refuse to believe, as so many Christians do, that it is all a device of the Devil, from which we demand prompt and immediate release.

Put in the plainest possible words let me show you what I mean.

First, my Father permits it to purge me and purify my character so that I can partake of His own impeccable character and conduct.

Second, He uses pain as a prod that pushes me out of a phony world into close communion with Himself.

I learned long ago not to demand deliverance from disease, pain, suffering, or adversity. So many contemporary Christians insist on instant healing. They are urged by their leaders and denominational emphasis to get their miracle from God—now—as though it is something to brag about.

This is very dangerous.

A classic illustration in God's record of how He deals with some diseases is that of King Hezekiah. Here was the most honorable monarch ever to rule over God's people. Up to the hour that he was stricken with terminal illness, Hezekiah had a reasonable record of bringing his nation back to God and conducting himself with the utmost dignity.

Had he consented to God's decision that the time had come for him to die, Hezekiah would have gone down in history as the most impeccable monarch to ever rule among men. Instead he demanded to be healed. He insisted on his miracle. He refused to accept God's will in the matter. As a result, he was granted another fifteen years of life.

Those were dreadful, dark, disastrous years for Hezekiah. Not just for him but for his entire family, for his nation, and for the honor of the Lord. Because of his intransigence, pride and arrogance came into his character. He became haughty because of his health and wealth (sound familiar?). Read for yourself in 2 Chronicles 32:22–35 the terrible tragedies that came upon this once magnificent man who demanded deliverance from his disease.

So, as I lay in that dark, damp room it came to me clearly that I should quietly rest in my Father's supernatural care. The calm assurance came to me that if He chose to restore my strength and energy, He could easily do so in ways unknown to me. He had done this often before and He could do it again. I also realized that if He wished to call me home, I was willing and ready to go. I did not wish my departure to be delayed.

He knew what was best. I would rest. This was the way to triumph against this time of trouble.

Chapter Ten

Cheri Is Stricken

Anyone who has read this far in the book will realize by now that the more endearing name that I use for Ursula is "Cheri." Perhaps this should have been explained earlier in this account. In any event, what we were soon to face was not only tough, but also, at times, rather hilarious—especially in retrospect.

Both of us were exceedingly grateful to our Father that Cheri was spared from any initial illness. This meant that with her energy and drive she could readily walk to the nearby stores to purchase anything we might need to keep us going. Both of us saw this as a great blessing.

Cheri comes from the "old school" that holds to the implicit belief that the best defense against disease is good nourishing food and a full stomach. She spared no pains or cash to purchase wholesome, nourishing items that she was sure would keep her well and contribute to my own recovery, though at this point food and drink held no interest whatever for me.

This is an appropriate time and place to recount just a little of Ursula's childhood in northern Germany. Then the reader will better understand the difficulties we were to face. Ursula, at the tender age of two years, lost her mother to tuberculosis.

Unable to care for this tiny tot properly, her father decided to place her in an excellent Christian orphanage, run by the Evangelical Lutheran Church. This institution was to be her home for the next twelve years of her life.

It was soon apparent to the staff that the little girl had a chest condition that predisposed her to lung disease, especially the dreaded tuberculosis. Her own older brother had died with this malady. So every summer she was sent off to stay in the countryside where the fresh air, sunshine, and fresh farm food could fortify her constitution. The treatment worked well. She became a keen athlete, able to run like a young gazelle.

Nevertheless, her susceptible chest condition never completely left her. The result has been that even well into her adult life she quickly succumbed to bronchitis whenever her health deteriorated. Again and again we had gone through some grim sessions when her vitality dropped dangerously low. So it can be understood why we were so grateful that she was well enough to be up and on her feet at a time when I was so ill.

But then, one dark, dreary morning everything changed very suddenly. I had not slept well. Throughout the long night, wracked with pain, I listened to a Pacific storm pound the ground with driving rain. The eave troughs on our building were blocked with masses of dead leaves and pine needles. Rivers of water cascaded down onto the patios and now we were like a little island surrounded by water.

The suite that we occupied, at the best of times, had virtually no sun coming through the windows because large trees shaded us. So the rooms were dark and damp—much more so than we had ever anticipated.

It was then, just before daybreak, when an even more ominous sound than the storm came from the adjoining bedroom. Cheri had started to cough. For most people that does not seem too serious. For us it spelled big trouble. We had been through the battles with major bronchitis before. But this struggle was to be complicated with another virus infection that would lay her low overnight.

In a matter of days I had a very, very ill woman beside me. We were a bit like a couple of scarecrows, both of us almost dead on our feeble feet. It was well nigh comical how we each tried to care for the other, only to collapse in weakness and dizziness.

Once Cheri went to the kitchen to prepare a cup of tea. All she had managed to do was turn on the stove before she was overcome with vertigo and collapsed into a chair. I then hobbled over to help and felt myself fainting with the effort. We were a couple of wounded old birds flopping around with bedraggled feathers and not much life.

Ursula now collapsed on the couch. It was my turn to see if I could summon some aid. Gathering up all my grit, I walked through the rain to the nearest telephone to call an elderly physician I had met in Santa Barbara years before. He was most cordial but explained that he had retired from practice, and in California no retired doctor is allowed to see a patient, make a diagnosis, or even write a prescription. I was exasperated.

Before I left the suite, Cheri and I had entreated our Father to guide me clearly in what do. Suddenly it seemed that I was up against a stone wall—a bit like Jericho's. There was silence on the phone, then the doctor spoke again.

"Phillip, there is actually a very good general practitioner who has his office just across the street from where you are staying." It seemed almost too good to be true just then. "Go and see him. Tell him I sent you. Tell him your trouble with Ursula. I am sure he will come to see her."

With that I was gone. I stumbled clumsily into the doctor's office—clothes all askew and damp from the rain—looking like a lost refugee. To my astonishment a huge man was right beside the door as if awaiting my arrival. In an outburst, I asked if he was the doctor. Yes, he was. Casting myself on his mercy I begged him to come with me. True to form, like an old-fashioned family doctor, he tossed a few instruments in his black bag, and within five minutes we stood beside Ursula's heaving body.

Instantly, he knew the problem. In moments he was done and ready to depart. I stopped him at the door, overwhelmed with gratitude. I insisted on paying at once. He paused a moment, looked at me hard, then quoted a figure that completely emptied my wallet.

When he was gone, I whispered to Ursula, "How can these doctors make so much money so quickly with any sort of clear conscience?" It was an unanswered question that simply hung suspended in space.

For us, on this difficult day, the great, giant man was our Father's provision in the time of trouble. Both of us were humbly grateful that he was genial enough to come to our home in an hour of need—just another one of those dear angels in disguise.

This episode virtually exhausted the last resources of energy in my battered old body. Allow me to respectfully remind the reader that I am in my seventy-fourth year, so there were no youthful resources to call upon. Only Christ remained. He heard this weak man's feeble cry of faith: *O Master, I do believe. But help Thou my unbelief.*

Bit by bit, from then on, I began to detect an element of hope that things might turn around. We might just stumble over some remedy to speed our recovery. We might just make it back from the brink to fight again another day. My hope was in Him.

It became increasingly evident to me that from all outward appearances we were in dire circumstances, but within there was the calm conviction that all would be well. Our predicament was in fact a part of our Father's plan and purpose to accomplish great, good benefits in our lives. His ways are not our ways. His thoughts are far above our thoughts. He could deliver us from all this trouble in triumph.

Just because there was so much adversity does not meat that we were out of His will. No, we were not the victims of bad luck or wrong choices. Rather we were His children in His care who could calmly count on Christ to make us victorious in the time of trouble. He was with us. All would be well.

It is quite astonishing how much trouble can pile up at times like this. To compound our concerns, it became evident that our mail was not getting through to us properly. We had paid a very substantial fee to have all our correspondence forwarded to us promptly. But it simply was not happening.

Of course one hears such awful horror stories about postal services these days that it was not difficult to imagine the worst. Still we tried to be patient and hoped ardently that any day things would turn around. But they seemed to get worse. This reminded me of the then-current joke that the increase in postage rates was to help cover storage costs.

It was now very close to Christmas—a time when mail is usually bountiful. But for us it was not to be. In fact, never in all my life had so much mail been lost. Once again, instead of our becoming angry and outraged, I urged Ursula to simply accept this as part of the profound lessons we were learning.

As a footnote to this trial it must be reported that one remarkable aspect was that eventually every piece of essential business correspondence did arrive. Oh, there were weeks and weeks of delay. Some of the letters had been torn open, but the contents were still intact. Parcels had been damaged but still came through. The truly grievous thing was that roughly one-third of our Christmas cards never came at all. No doubt they ended up in a dumpster, tossed there by some carrier, too tired to pack his heavy bag any longer. In fact, one case was reported at that time that a letter carrier, weary of so much work, simply rented a huge storage locker and there deposited the offending mail. It all seemed so strange and unreal in a society where we pride ourselves on our communication expertise. At least we learned to laugh lightheartedly about our losses. Surely it was better to laugh than to cry and rage against adversity.

Another amusing adventure was how we got help when we were in need of supplies. There was no telephone in our unit. So we would both stagger out to the street. Then I would ask Cheri to lean against the stone wall surrounding our compound. From that vantage point she could keep an eye on me, making sure that I did not collapse along the way, while I crossed the road to a friend's office in a nearby building.

Our logic was that if either one of us fainted in this venture, then one of us would be there to pick the other up and help get them home. Meanwhile, over at the office, I would leave a little note with one or two items to be picked up at the store in due course. It all sounds a bit weird and wacky in modern-day America, but that is how we beat the odds against us without going to the hospital or being a burden to others.

Whenever we recall those difficult days, it is indeed astonishing how we now laugh hilariously over our antics. Some of our friends and even some of our neighbors must have thought we were an odd couple. But for us, meeting the challenge was an elixir that spurred us on.

Gradually it became apparent that Ursula was making a more rapid recovery from her illness than I was. Of course she had the advantage of being younger, and she did not have the crippling effect of painful joints and a bad back that bowed my body beyond my ability to move properly. So it was wonderful to see her spry again.

Then an incident took place that was to change the whole course of our lives. Often our Father uses the common things to touch us in the most uncommon ways. I have sometimes called them God's beautiful bonuses for His children—especially for those of us who trust Him in childlike simplicity. Somehow we are alert, awake, and waiting quietly for Him to open the way before us. And He does!

Our dear, dear friend who had brought us the extra pots and pans, kitchenware, and bedding dropped in to see us. She was brave to do this for we knew not how contagious our disease might be. She is a very gentle lady—gracious, thoughtful, and caring. She sat down near me, still prostrate on the couch, and quietly asked me to describe to her all my symptoms.

When I was done with my somewhat discouraging account, she looked at me with enormous empathy. "That is exactly what I went through several months ago." I could scarcely believe her. She went on to tell us how she sought the finest medical advice in the city, submitted to every possible test by the specialists, and endured many X-rays, all to no avail. Her condition, identical to mine, became more acute and she was sent home to endure the agony without any remedy.

One day in absolute anguish she flung herself across her bed, head almost touching the floor for some slight relief, she cried out to Christ for help. In an instant there flashed through her mind, like a brilliant light, the memory of a dear, dear old gentleman well into his nineties who was spry, nimble, and a great blessing to the many shut-ins whom he visited.

It was her gracious generosity that made his visitation possible for she drove him from home to home on his missions of mercy. Every once in a while she would be asked to take him to a health-food shop where he picked up a large bottle of alfalfa pills. His comment simply was, "They keep me going."

On this dreadful day the thought that came to her was simply: *Try the same treatment.* She did. Within a month her pains began to diminish, and her mobility returned. Now she sat beside me completely restored. "Phillip," she said softly, "why don't you do the same? Try the alfalfa."

It was a direct word from our Father. Without delay I got in an ample stock of alfalfa pills. Today I am completely renewed. Jokingly I tell my friends, "I decided to go back to the hearty old ranch feed that I ate before I was put out to pasture!"

Thank you, Father!

Chapter Eleven

The Messiah

The renewal of my health, which began in that simple but beautiful way, remains a memorial to the unfailing goodness of God, My Father. When He sent His Son to become the Holy Anointed One, the Most High, the Messiah, the Living Christ among us, it was not only to be our Savior. It was also to set us free from our diseases, our dilemmas, and our difficulties.

This tremendous truth, this incredible insight, this acute inner assurance burned intensely in my conscience. *Phillip, you were brought to Santa Barbara to this little suite to find a simple, sure cure for the condition that has caused you so much suffering for so many years.*

Such are the ways of God—so simple, so plain, and so profound. His thoughts are not our thoughts, all tied up in technology.

> . . . I am the LORD that healeth thee (Ex. 15:26).

Now, more than ever before, I know this to be so.

In humility, in honor, and in awe I bow before Him.

He can, and He does, make all things new.

When I staggered into the health shop to ask for alfalfa, the young woman in charge looked at me with compassion. "All crippled up with acute arthritis?" she asked softly.

"I don't really know what it is," I replied a bit embarrassed. "A friend said that alfalfa would help, and I believe her!"

The lady handed me a huge bottle of alfalfa pills. "You are an old gentleman, badly crippled, I'll give you a generous discount." She handed me the bottle with a smile. "This is the best-kept health secret in America."

I staggered home all smiles. Time would soon prove her right.

The alfalfa cure was just like the Good News of our Father's great love for lost men and women. It was almost too simple, too easy, too wonderful to be true or laid hold of in faith. Yes, yes, He has such gracious, unexpected, wondrous ways to provide for His people in their hour of peril. He is able to do far beyond whatever we might ever imagine.

About this time some dear friends dropped in to see if we felt fit enough to attend a performance of the *Messiah.* Up until then, there had been neither the strength or the vitality to go to any social event. But just the mention of the *Messiah* was enough for me to gather up all the courage I could and decide to go.

There is a profound power in that magnificent and majestic music. The message in that great oratorio is the grandest spiritual theme in all the universe. It is Christ's coming to earth to be both our Savior and our Shepherd. It is His love overcoming our despair, His light dispelling our darkness, His life triumphing against our death.

No music in all the world has ever moved me in the same manner as has the *Messiah.* Often I am amazed at its splendid grandeur and the stirring glory that it bestows on our gracious God. No other piece of sacred music can begin to approach its power. Often I wonder to myself why it is that contemporary composers of the twentieth century have never even come close to matching its magnificence.

It is a masterpiece that bows my spirit before the Messiah.

It is a composition that exalts Christ in noble tones.

It is an oratorio of majesty and might that stirs my whole being in honor and praise to Him.

It was not always so in my life!

There was a time, as a young man, that I found this composition ponderous, heavy, and rather boring. That was before I came into a vital, dynamic, life-changing encounter with the living Christ—Messiah Himself. Then suddenly the music and the message of this magnificent work impacted me with remarkable power.

It never ceases to astound me how our Father uses our days of distress and despair to bring us His supernatural life.

The *Messiah* itself was a case in point of this profound principle. As we eagerly anticipated going to this special event, there came back to me with inspiring clarity the first time that the *Messiah* spoke to my spirit in preparation for my remarkable encounter with Christ Himself.

This was almost exactly thirty-three years before. I had been laid low by a violent attack of malaria. Then, as now, I was prostrate on a couch in the country kitchen in the ranch house that we then occupied. It was a time of great trouble, for I had a large ranch to manage. Haying season was at its peak, but not a thing could be done. I was flat on my back, weak and helpless.

A neighboring rancher, some four miles up the road, heard about my plight on the back-country grapevine. To my unbounded surprise he showed up at our house one hot summer morning. He had come to put up my hay! What a generous fellow.

More than that, he brought with him his collection of records, including the *Messiah*. "Just listen to this magnificent music, Phillip. It will lift your spirits. Take in the words, too, they will get your mind off all your troubles."

Out of gratitude for all his kindness, I did exactly what the tough little rancher told me to do. I played those records over and over and over, and in the playing not only did the generosity and glory of God's grace begin to prepare my hard heart to meet Christ in person that fall season, but it also began to heal and bind up my disease-battered body.

Yes, our Father has His strong hands at work behind the scenes, amidst our adversity, to bring us great good. And as we anticipated hearing the *Messiah* once more, I was sure that it would be a special, special evening—a time that He would use to enable us to triumph against trouble.

The night of the performance, our friends came early to pick us up. I was glad of this because it would give us a better chance to find a suitable parking spot, as well as a close-up seat in the sanctuary. For years and years, I had longed to attend a live performance of the *Messiah*, with the special privilege of sitting close to the choir and orchestra. I was sure that to be in intimate proximity to the music itself would provide a powerful new dimension to the rendition.

When we pulled into the church yard, it appeared almost empty. There were only a handful of vehicles there. But soft lights glowed from the Spanish-style structure. It was an aged building of great dignity, decorated very simply but tastefully with brilliant red poinsettias. The scarlet, rich foliage was a perfect foil for the cream-colored walls.

We appeared to be the very first to arrive, so the choice of seats was glorious. I approached a middle-aged man, who appeared to be the conductor, and asked if he had any objection to our sitting up at the very front, almost among the choir members. He replied that that was fine, and he was glad to have us there.

The entire setting was so simple, so unsophisticated.

I loved the low lights that warmed the plain walls.

A quiet hush pervaded the place as people came in.

Stillness and a sacred serenity settled over us.

The church had not engaged high-profile performers to impress the audience. Instead, they were simply allowing their own regular choir members to lift their voices in praise. This was not to be a performance to entertain us. Rather it would be a sincere celebration to recount the coming of Christ into our weary world. It was a night again to give great glory, great honor, and great exaltation to the Most High who lives, rules, and presides over us in majesty, might, peace, and power.

I could scarcely restrain myself in eager anticipation.

Soon the members of the instrumental ensemble filed in. My spirit was saddened for a few moments. They seemed so elderly, so lined with years under the southern sun, and so few in number. Little did I know how those venerable veterans could set their strings to singing in magnificent harmony. As so often happens in spiritual matters, it is not a question of size or scale or sensationalism that counts but rather the sincere earnestness of a soul centered in Christ. And here were a handful of musicians who obviously played out of profound love for our Lord.

Their music was inspired by the Most High.

They were not trying to impress us but played to praise Him.

The presence of God was among us!

The choir took its place. Plain people—members of this congregation—who can be found in almost any church, but with one distinguishing difference—there was an aura of peace, quiet serenity, and inner joy on their countenances.

They were so close that I could read every face.

This was not just another recital.

This was a celebration to honor our God.

The strains of the music swelled in majestic harmony to fill the entire sanctuary. It was as if I was at the very center of its creation. Never in all my life had such an aura of awe and wonder and pure inspiration engulfed my soul from the *Messiah*. This must have been akin to the vision and splendor that had come upon Handel during those days in which he composed this masterpiece. Truly, truly the hand of the Most High was guiding every impulse of his spirit, for there sprang forth a work that has moved millions of men and women in thousands of places all across the earth.

To my amazement I felt as though I was actually a member of the choral group itself. It seemed that I could not remain silent. I was caught up in the pure joy of giving praise to Christ for coming among us—not only at Bethlehem, but also on this memorable night in Santa Barbara.

His presence pervaded this simple sanctuary.

His power swept into our souls.

His peace ignited our spirits.

No wonder the angel of the Lord came to the terrified shepherds outside of Bethlehem.

> Fear not: for, behold, I bring you good tidings of great joy, which shall be to all people. For unto you is born this day in the city of David a Saviour, which is Christ the Lord. Glory to God in the highest and on earth peace, good will toward men (Luke 2:10–11, 14).

That wondrous night was more than a single incident in the remarkable history of Christ's coming to earth. It was happening again on this winter night in this Spanish-style sanctuary by the sea. It had happened again and again and again all across the earth to thousands of people humble in heart, willing to receive the King of Glory as their Messiah.

In a deeply moving way, I knew this night that He had come to us in incredible intimacy. As of old, He reassured us not to fear despite all the trouble. He was bringing us good tidings of great joy that could triumph over every trial. He would honor Himself in the midst of our turmoil by bringing His peace, His strength, and His tranquillity.

Christ does just that when we expose all to Him.

He quietly enters into every area opened to Him.

His presence speaks serenity within.

He comes in good will.

All is well.

That evening He touched me, and I began to heal.

As we rose to leave the simple sanctuary, the friend who brought us over in his car spoke to me very earnestly, "Phillip, I have listened to this music all my life. But tonight, for the first time, it all came together. Now I fully understand its majestic message."

He too had been touched by the Most High.

For both of us it was an evening that we would never forget.

It had been an interval of glorious inspiration.

Actually it was like a turning point, a hinge if you will, upon which the remaining events of this trouble-filled winter would turn, and turn out to be truly wonderful. In the day-to-day events that were to follow, we could see how incident upon incident was ordained by our Father to serve His purposes for us. But, equally energizing, they had all been planned and prepared to be His chariots and horsemen sent to preserve us from despair.

As in the days of Elisha, what I needed was to have my spiritual vision cleared so that I could see emphatically that Christ Himself was present and powerful in every situation—no matter how severe. Elisha had cried out for his servant,

> . . . the LORD opened the eyes of the young man; and he

> saw: and, behold, the mountain was full of horses and chariots of fire round about . . . (2 Kings 6:17).

It demands implicit, childlike trust in Christ to call out like this in the midst of much trouble, but little by little I am learning that whatever element of faith I need to have for complete confidence in Christ must come from His own life—in other words His own faith—being exercised in me hour by hour.

It is His might, His power, His presence, His peace, His faith, and His calm confidence that overcomes the world. I am totally dependent upon Him to accomplish His own good purposes within me as well as in the world around me.

He put it plainly, "without Me you can do nothing."

But also I know that "with God, all things are possible."

Bless His Name!

Chapter Twelve

Dear, Dear Friends

It will be recalled that our original thought in going to California for the winter was to find a very quiet spot where I could write without disturbance. To that end we had tried to find accommodation somewhere along the more sparsely settled central coast. It was not meant to be.

Our Father in His infinite wisdom and full foreknowledge knew of our impending illnesses. So, in His remarkable mercy and kindness He led us on to locate in the New Horizons just northwest of Santa Barbara. This in truth, and in practical reality, was His place gently prepared for us.

It was still my sincere hope and earnest desire to get a new manuscript under way. Little did I realize at the outset of my great illness how severe it would be or how long it would last. Because of my desire to write, we intended to try and spend our time in California very quietly, away from undue social activities. By choice we did not have a telephone installed in the suite simply because it would give some relief from the constant demands made upon me to meet speaking engagements, and so forth.

In one way this served its purpose very well indeed. We did enjoy more seclusion and privacy. That alone was a decided benefit. But there was a second, much more precious, result of being without a phone. It was simply this: If people really wanted to see us they simply had to come over for a visit in person. It was like turning back the clock of contemporary civilization to phone-free days, back to the pioneer times when people cared enough about each other to actually visit in person. This meant that one had to drop what they were doing and set aside a bit of time for a friend or neighbor—to go over and "sit a bit." This entailed a bit of sacrifice. What astonished us with pure, unalloyed joy was the manner in which our friends did just that for us. Hardly a day passed but there would be a gentle knock on the door, a surprise visit, and the pure pleasure of having a friend come in for a chat and a cup of tea.

In reminiscing over the events of that tough winter, these frequent and happy interludes with our friends stand out as something very, very sweet and reassuring, partly, I suppose, because I am very much an old-fashioned man who revels in the simple joys of life. I am very pleasantly satisfied with the clasp of a warm hand, the sincere smile of someone fond of me, the hearty hug of a friend, the lighthearted laughter that comes in happy company, the shared stories of our life's great adventure with God, and just the deep delight of speaking sincerely of Christ's care for us.

None of this pleasure is planned or programmed. These are the bounties that come to us in abundance when we take time for each other. And I give it here as a living testimony to our dear, dear friends in Santa Barbara that they truly enriched our weeks there in loving and wondrous ways just by coming to visit. The memory of those moments is like a golden glow that enfolds us in love and gentle kindness.

We Christians speak much about "being touched" by Christ. It is a phrase that sounds so spiritual, so sanctimonious. Yet, its practical reality is worked out in the daily encounters that we enjoy with His children. It is so often through their kind actions, their caring concern, their generous gestures, and their love and encouragement that we are "touched" by our Father. This amazing demonstration of His care for us helped us triumph against every trouble.

I remember the stormy, rainy day when I heard a faint knock on the door. I was not sure that there really was someone there, or if it was just my imagination, but I went anyway to see who the visitor might be. To my unbounded joy there was not just one person there, but *three*. A young father was all smiles and garbed in heavy, warm winter gear stood there with his two tiny tots. One was a wee girl with the face of an angel and the spirit to match. The little lad was all decked out like a little lumberjack and had the puckish grin of a little dynamo of mischief. It was his sister who had tapped so gently on the door.

They rushed over to hug me hard around my crippled old hips. The love, the warmth, and the innocent happiness that swept through me cannot be conveyed in words. They were full of chatter, excitement, goodwill, and great cheer.

Almost in unison and with breathless delight we hugged and hugged, laughed and laughed.

"Can we call you grandpa?"

Of course they could! I was enfolded in the love and the warmth and the pure ecstasy of their exuberance.

Behind them stood a handcart loaded with wood that their dad had cut at home.

"We've brought you wood for your fireplace to keep you warm this winter!"

I beamed with surprise.

In response, they jumped up and down, up and down, clapping their hands in glee.

Quickly they piled the wood in its huge box out on the patio. Then they were off for another load, and another, until the wood box was packed to capacity. They reminded me of squirrels packing away nuts against winter weather. They exhibited so much fun, so much laughter, and so much cheer.

Then, with the work all done, they came into our simple little suite to share some special treat that "Grandma" always has stashed away for special days.

These three dear, dear people knew how much I loved the open fire in our corner fireplace. They knew I would sit beside it, soak its warmth into my aching old joints, and slowly turn my back like an old tomcat to take its heat. They knew that on some nights, when it was unusually cool and damp, with frost on the grass and sleet on the shingles, I would curl up and sleep by that fire to give respite to my aching bones.

I positively refused to turn to medications.

So often, oh so often, I had seen the havoc that medicine had wreaked on others. No indeed, if I was to get well, it would have to be with natural means provided by My Father and also with the loving touch of His hand through my friends.

The noble, grand lesson that I was learning so clearly in this time of trouble was that He was actively engaged in all our affairs, bringing enormous benefits to us out of apparent adversity. We need that lesson over and over and over. Most of the arrogant Western world needs to be reminded again and again and again that affluence, independence, and apparent control of our lives are just not enough for abundant living.

We need the Most High. We need His people. We need the wonders and inspiration of His creation. We need each other.

Yet, so many of us withhold love from each other.

Somehow our society spurns a show of affection.

Our people prefer to think it is "cool" to be aloof.

All of us are much more the poorer for it.

But happily for Ursula and myself just the opposite was true during this long and slow convalescence. We were shown a level of concern, care, and old-fashioned compassion that set my spirit singing and set my soul at ease. This outpouring of practical love satisfied me that life, despite the tough times, was still well worth living—even for a disabled old codger like myself.

Day after day there was someone at the door.

Just to have someone drop in for a wee chat was a love gift.

I say that in all sincerity, for it means that a man or woman cares enough to take the time, the trouble, and the thought to turn their attention to someone else who is in need. In short, it is a sacrifice of one's self to reach out and actually perform this act of mercy and kindness. It is a much more profound and generous gesture than merely picking up the phone with a flip of the wrist and spending two whole minutes in empty chatter from the convenience of your armchair.

Occasionally, truly hilarious incidents took place during those unexpected visits. One I shall never forget. It is recounted here to convey, tongue in cheek, the fun we had with our friends.

It was a glorious, warm, sunny afternoon. I longed to get out and stretch my body in the sun. From my earliest childhood in Kenya I had always turned to the sun for healing and help. The Africans did it, the dogs all did it, the chickens all did it, the wildlife did it—all loved it. So why should I not do it?

There was a small patch of brilliant sunlight that fell on the enclosed patio just outside the front door. It was only there a couple of hours, streaming in between the trees and a magnificent bougainvillea vine that adorned the balcony above us in scarlet splendor. It was a first, hesitant effort to get out and stretch myself in the warm rays. So, stripped down to only a brief pair of shorts, I tossed a blanket in the spot of warm sunlight and lay down flat on my face and chest. In amazing relief, with the sun so warm on my back and legs, I was asleep in minutes.

Ursula had slipped over to the shops on one of her little shopping sprees, so it was a choice time to rest—or so I thought. I had been asleep only a few minutes when the latch on the patio gate rattled and woke me. Still half asleep, without turning over, I assumed that Ursula was back early.

"Come in darling." I called out softly. There was no reply, so I drowsily assumed that she did not wish to disturb my siesta in the sun. I continued to rest face down.

Then I heard a soft voice just beside me. It was not my wife's familiar tones. A bit startled I opened my eyes and looked up. There crouched down on the patio floor right beside me was a dear, dear lady, even more aged than I, who has been a special friend for over forty years.

She was all smiles, a twinkle of mischief in her eyes. "It is me, Phillip," she chuckled gleefully—not a bit embarrassed by my scanty attire. "I brought over this package of mail for you."

Both of us had a hearty laugh over my predicament. I urged her to come inside while I dressed somewhat sheepishly, but with all the speed I could muster. I quickly prepared a cup of tea and was just ready to serve my special guest when Ursula came home. All of us erupted in gales of laughter over this episode. That high humor and wholesome goodwill was a better medication than anything any doctor could prescribe, of that I was sure.

This dear person also came with generous gifts of sweet mandarins, avocados, oranges, and lemons grown in their garden. Her husband, at eighty-four, is still an active landscape gardener, an amazing man of gentle words and gentle spirit.

We literally feasted and feasted on the bounties of fresh fruit so many of our friends brought to out little suite. There was not just one bowl heaped with the delicious produce from their trees, but three of them. Wherever one turned there was an abundance of glorious, golden, fresh fruit at hand for the taking. Ursula and I reveled in it all, sure that all of its sweetness would do us great good. One visitor even commented on how we arranged the fruit in such artistic art forms. All of it was helping to heal us.

Another gesture that did us so much great good was the way in which our friends came over to take us out on little drives, or little walks, or little shopping trips for Ursula. She just loved those little outings. She has become a very shrewd shopper. She knows values and when she comes across a truly sensational purchase she is all smiles. It is as if she has achieved a triumph in trade. So she bears her booty home in honor and joy to share it with me.

As little by little, week by week, my vitality began to return, I found real pleasure in these little jaunts with our friends. Swiftly and smoothly, they would whisk us across town in the heavy traffic to spend precious hours in their homes or at some special service. They were doing their utmost to lift up the fallen, to reintroduce us again into the stream of life, and to reengage us in the joys of human interaction.

I could see and sense this in a remarkable manner. They really did want me well again. As one man said to me in utter sincerity when he saw my bony, skinny condition, "Phillip you have always seemed so fit, so energetic, so strong." Then with utmost empathy he added, "We're just going to get you back there again with God's help!"

That is strong medicine indeed for a weak man who is struggling to regain his strength. It was like music coming through this humble, hearty fellow from our Father's heart. Yes, yes I did believe that I would get back to health with so much love.

Dear friends gave us a radio to tune in a fine music station.

They loaned us a TV set so we could watch the Winter Olympics. They brought us magnificent magazines, beautiful books, lovely plants, and bouquets of flowers to brighten our humble home. They came with casseroles, delectable dishes, and special snacks to strengthen us.

But best of all they brought themselves. It was their affection, their warmth, their prayers, and their simple faith in Christ that all would be well that counted so much to me.

Dear, dear friends! Precious, precious people!

Chapter Thirteen

The Will to Be Well

As the winter season moved steadily into the new year it became increasingly clear to me that my own recovery would be slow and prolonged. There would be no so-called quick fix. Whatever the true nature of the malady that afflicted me, it had done enormous damage that would require a long, slow convalescence. To be open and honest with the reader, it must be stated here that though I had fetched a doctor to prescribe some antibiotics for Ursula, I did not consult him about my own condition. The reasons for this decision are very personal and long standing. They have been stated in detail in previous books such as *Taming Tension* and *Wonder O' the Wind.*

But, undergirding my own health there lies a profound unshakable confidence in Christ to care for me amid adversity. Again and again I place my whole person—body, soul, and spirit—in His keeping. My implicit confidence is that despite a frail body and fragile health He could sustain me in strength sufficient to serve Him and His people until He calls me home.

This should not be construed as demanding a disease-free life. I have lived long enough to have seen some of His choicest children endure great suffering and succumb. What I ask for is simply the energy and vitality to survive the slings and stones of adversity with courage enough to carry out my duties and still bring honor to Him during whatever span of life He gives me.

This same request can be found in the Psalms.

> I am as a wonder unto many; but thou art my strong refuge. Let my mouth be filled with thy praise and with thy honour all the day. Cast me not off in the time of old age; forsake me not when my strength faileth (Ps. 71:7–9).

> Now also when I am old and grayheaded, O God, forsake me not; until I have shewed thy strength unto this generation, and thy power to every one that is to come (Ps. 71:18).

There it is in the plainest possible terms.

There is no personal pride, only total trust in Christ.

There is the determined desire only to honor Him. My own will to get well was precisely the same. This I was determined to do.

It would call for quiet faith in God my Father.

It would call for calm acceptance of long delays.

It would call for sure self-discipline.

I knew from long experience that He would be faithful in honoring my complete confidence in Him. My part was to reciprocate by complying with whatever measures He meted out to me for recovery.

In a previous chapter I recounted how our friend told us about the alfalfa treatment. I was determined to take this simple remedy with unfailing regularity. Unlike so many patients who hop, skip, and jump around from one medication to another, this was a course of action that I would persevere with until it worked wonders to my well-being.

Like so many natural cures, it seemed almost too simple, too old-fashioned, too much like the farm, or too fanciful. But, having loved the land all my life, such diatribes did not put me off. Alfalfa for centuries has been called "the father of all feeds" because of its high nutritional content so beneficial to livestock.

The alfalfa plant, native to the Arabian deserts, is a deep-rooted plant of enormous vigor. Its roots will go down twenty feet through the most unfavorable terrain searching out nutrients, minerals, and trace elements that are incorporated into its foliage. Little wonder that it is in fact a wonder food.

Without fuss or fanfare, I simply stuck to the regime of taking these huge tablets morning and evening. For the first four weeks there was no perceptible change in my condition. But it was a remedy brought to me in such a remarkable but simple way, so I was not going to give up.

Then one sunny, happy, bright morning I staggered out the door for a wee walk around the grounds. At once I sensed that I could actually straighten my back a bit. As I did so, it was exciting to realize that the excruciating pains had begun to relent. I was amazed and ecstatic! When I returned, I shared the wondrous good news with Cheri. Then she, too, burst into radiant smiles that lit up her entire countenance with good cheer.

This incident exactly resembled the first, faint hint of spring. It was like a bright ray of fresh hope bursting on the horizon. Help was on the way. Healing and restoration were in this day. The encouragement that this brought is hard to describe. But one thing it did was to redouble my determination to do whatever I could to get well.

One thing that I could do was to find the very finest, wholesome, fresh fruit and vegetables. Happily, the Goleta area has always been famous for its fertile farmland. It still has its share of family farms where local people grow fruit and vegetables of exceptional quality. Many of them use only organic methods, free from chemical fertilizers or poisonous pesticides.

Best of all, every Thursday afternoon, at exactly 3:00 P.M. sharp, the farmer's market would open for business. This would be announced by the ringing of a handbell. Ursula and I went there with friends. It was less than a mile from where we stayed, and soon we were bearing home great bulging bags of glorious, fresh, wholesome produce picked that day. It was all a joyous adventure to try new fruits, rare roots, vegetables, nuts, and even wild honey.

Our diet was enriched beyond measure by this little farmer's market—just another one of those beautiful bonuses bestowed on us in love by our Father. I even enjoyed chatting with the growers, most of whom were strong, healthy, sun-browned people who loved their land and loved their life and loved to share the fruit of their labor with us.

For example, one genial fellow did not sell us just plain old Brussels sprouts. He carefully lifted each entire plant out of the rich soil. They were washed meticulously and then sold in their entirety. And they were huge, about three feet tall. He took the trouble to explain that we could use all the giant leaves as a green, superior to any spinach. Then there were the masses of tightly packed sprouts, each one perfect and fresh for picking. Finally there remained the thick, edible stalk that was equal to any celery and enough to provide us with at least four hearty meals all for just one dollar.

Are you surprised that we began to share such secrets with our friends? Even they were surprised with what we brought home. I went crazy over the dark, rich honey gathered from the wild flowers and flowering desert shrubs of California. Again, it too, was about half the price of regular processed honey. It was truly tasty, pungent with the potency of wild nectar produced under the warm southern sun.

Speaking of the sun, this, too, was to play its part in contributing to my recovery. From the years of my earliest boyhood in Kenya I had always been impressed with the way in which every well and ill being loved to bask in the sun. They would stretch themselves in its gentle warmth, both morning and evening, to soak up the life-giving rays. It is a special pleasure that I have enjoyed all my life. If done in moderation, avoiding the heat of the day, it can be most beneficial. It is one of the Father's gentle gifts to His children. Best of all it was free for the taking.

One of the great benefits in staying at the New Horizons was the free use of their magnificent, heated outdoor pool. Because most of the residents were elderly people, the water was kept at a soothing 84°F. Even on cool windy days it was warm enough to be inviting. Often I was the only one who would be there to get regular exercise.

Somehow I was absolutely sure that diligent swimming in the warm water would do much to help limber up my body and restore flexibility to my painful joints. At times it took grim determination and resolve to drag myself over there. It was not always the easiest regime. But, if it would help I was determined to do it, even if my back, legs, and shoulder muscles screamed for relief.

It astonished me, in speaking to some of the other people who came to the pool, how highly they praised this therapy. One or two claimed that they were severely crippled before coming the New Horizons to live and swim. With perseverance and some pain, the regular use of the pool had restored their mobility, and they were not ashamed to say so with deep conviction.

Week after week I would walk over for my workout. Week after week the warm water worked its wonders. Week after week sore muscles, stiff joints, and tortured tendons began to loosen and heal.

Probably the best part of all was when I stretched out in the gentle winter sun afterward and just rested in its radiance. It was not strong enough to sear the skin, but warm enough to enfold my old beaten body in wonderful contentment. For all of these gentle benefits I was deeply grateful, sure that each was helping to heal my disease and restore my strength—all of them gracious gifts from my Father.

At times, especially when I lost so much weight, I must have looked a fright. Loose skin hanging on my bony body made me look like a famine refugee. But pride of appearance would not keep me from that pool.

I was touched by the fact that others who came to enjoy the warm waters did not shun me. Quite the contrary, they were cordial and friendly, even though I was a newcomer and only a temporary resident. One of these was a little man, exactly my own age, who came in his wheelchair. He, too, like me, was of hardy Swiss stock. Unfortunately he had suffered a massive stroke and half his body was paralyzed, leaving him not only crippled but also unable to speak.

Somehow a real bond of affinity began to build between us. Of course he had no way of communicating with me, except through hand gestures and the expression on his face. But one of his family told me what an active and virile person he had been all his life. He had served as a Swiss mountain guide and ski instructor until his seventies. Then, apparently in perfect health, he quietly went to bed one night, woke up about 2:00 A.M., and found himself stricken with this massive stroke. What a shock for someone so fit!

He would wheel himself over beside me and the two of us would just stretch ourselves in the sun and quietly relish each other's companionship. Both of us understood implicitly that we were locked in a battle to get back our strength, our stamina, and our mobility. There passed between us the mutual understanding and encouragement of kindred spirits. No need to speak much, just be there for each other.

One afternoon, to my utter astonishment, the little man stood up right in front of me. He could only hold himself there a few seconds, but it was a major breakthrough, a triumph of the will. I could not contain myself for joy! I congratulated him on this achievement. He beamed back, all smiles, his eyes shining with new resolve. From then on he began to stand more and more often, for longer and longer periods of time. We were both gaining ground, winning the war of our wills, and determined to recover.

Across the years, Christ has brought home to me the dear and unshakable conviction that to be a holy person is to be a wholesome person. That is to say, whole in spirit, whole in soul, and whole in body. This statement is easy to write down on paper, but it is one of the most challenging to carry out in real life.

In our contemporary society where popular thinking is so largely dominated by those who utterly ignore the spiritual dimension of life, the above sentiments are considered absurd. For example, so many who turn to the medical profession for remedies seldom seem to be aware that it takes more than doctors or drugs to make them whole. Also involved are our attitudes, our emotions, our wills—our soul life. But beyond even this lies the profound relationship we have with the living Christ who makes us whole in spirit.

Strange as it may seem, even people who have very little time for God will blame Him when things go wrong in their lives. They accuse Him of bringing the calamity upon them—as if the loving God was somehow a monster.

In my own case, in this prolonged time of trouble, again and again I entreated Him to examine and search my innermost being. There was to be no resentment for my suffering, no hint of blaming another for my condition, no faultfinding with my lot in life. Rather it was to be accepted with grace as an experience in which He would again prove His unfailing faithfulness to me in my distress.

It was He who by His presence and by His power could work in me both to will and to do of His good pleasure. And a singular part of that work was to set my will to be well again. He could energize my will, strengthen my resolve, and quicken my faith to believe without my doubting that He could make me whole.

Little by little, bit by bit, and step-by-step it became apparent that my Father was working wonders in this ordeal—not just for my battered old body, but also for all my soul and all my spirit.

Chapter Fourteen

Thrill upon Thrill

Slowly, surely, and steadily my mobility was increasing. So too was my capacity to make short outings into the surrounding areas. When the days were fine and warm, I would drive the three miles down to the nearest beach to take long strolls along the shore. The ocean edge with its marvelous seascapes, its surging surf, its pure sea air, its delectable solitude, and its soaring birds had always worked wonders to my well-being. I have written much about the sea in such books as *Ocean Glory* and *Sea Edge*. The seashore has been a great place of healing, help, and wholeness for me.

And, in this time of trouble, it was again a special, special gift that my Father used to renew and restore my strength. It astonished me to no end how few people used the beaches in the winter. Many mornings I would encounter only one or two other people during my long hikes along the water's edge. More often than not they were solitary fishermen hoping to catch some fish from the swirling surf.

If the day was really warm, I would plunge my body into the breakers, dashing the strong sea water all over myself. It made my skin tingle with its pungency combined with a surge of rapid blood circulation. What a thrill! Then I would take shelter in some little cove or behind a pile of driftwood allowing the sun to warm me in its embrace. This was all a tremendous tonic that did a world of good.

Out on the great stretches of shining sand swept clean by the tumbling tides I would raise my spirit and my soul in joyous praise and hearty thanksgiving to Christ for all that He was accomplishing. In truth, in reality, in actual fact, He was making me whole. My strength was increasing. My energy was mounting. My hope was abounding. Once more my Father was demonstrating to me that He was totally trustworthy. In company with Him, it was possible to triumph against trouble. To Him went the honor.

Still, above and beyond my own personal renewal, there was deep within my spirit an undeniable conviction that Christ had brought us to this place for reasons not yet revealed to us. Our Father so often works quietly behind the scenes performing marvelous miracles on our behalf that eventually thrill us through and through. They are triumphs of His grace, demonstrations of His supremacy in all that concerns us.

Our part is to quietly count on His care and consistency.

Our walk with Him is not based on what we can observe.

Our companionship with Christ is grounded on His unshakable fidelity to us as His friends.

This is faith in action. It is faith in His character. It is faith in His unbreakable commitments to us as His people.

Soon I would see the actual working out of this profound, powerful principle in a most stirring little incident. Small in itself, perhaps, but mighty and majestic in its implications.

One sunny day I told Ursula that I felt strongly compelled to just drive across town and make my first visit of the season to our beloved rescue mission. It had been more than two years since I had last visited this work. I would just go quietly, unannounced, to see how the mission and its staff were progressing.

As I drove down, there moved through my mind a series of brief scenes—clear, sharp, and stirring—of our deep association with this endeavor across the years. It was like a replay of the past on a giant movie screen in my memory.

My initial great concern and compassion watching homeless young women with babies pawing through the city trash cans to find food to support their very lives. My pleading with the men at the small mission to enlarge the work to take in women and waifs.

My deep empathy for the destitute men whom I found sleeping on the beaches, in the bushes, and under culverts—street people without homes.

The long struggle with the city to gain a new location. The opposition of the local, wealthy people. The antagonism of the tourist industry. No one wanted an improved rescue mission in this affluent town.

Finally, our spirits ignited by the Spirit of Christ, in burning compassion, Ursula and I gave our home, in its lovely location near the sea, to break the logjam of opposition and procure a new location. It set off a chain reaction in the city. All sorts of different people suddenly came forward to offer their time, their skills, their help, and their money to make it happen. A magnificent new mission was built that would house scores of street people and provide shelter for unwed mothers and children.

Yes, yes, yes! In wondrous ways, a great and joyous work was underway. It served thousands upon thousands of needy souls. Hundreds and hundreds met Christ in this place.

But still it was a struggle to meet the enormous financial needs. Although I lived, now, some thirteen hundred miles away, I refused to relinquish our support for the work. We would do what we could to undergird this endeavor for God and for the lost. So far it had gone on for years. We would triumph with His might.

Now I was driving down to see how things were going.

I parked on a side street, locked the car, and went to see the completed work on the women's wing. It was handsome. "Thank you, Father," I spoke aloud in sincere gratitude.

Then I came around the new structure, and there standing outside the main entrance was the director's wife and the newly appointed chairman of the board. They simply could not believe that I had showed up suddenly by surprise—so unexpectedly.

There were warm hugs, radiant smiles, and animated, joyous conversation. They could hardly constrain themselves in sharing all the recent, great news of our Father's care.

- Some exceedingly wise, gifted, devout people had come forward to voluntarily join their staff in generous service. Now they had much more time to devote to touching individual lives for Christ.
- The building program was now virtually complete. All was well.
- An estate had been probated, leaving the mission with a handsome endowment that would cover their contingencies. Such joy!

As I drove home I was utterly ecstatic, thrill upon thrill! Now, suddenly, I understood clearly why once again my Father had arranged for us to be in Santa Barbara. Here in hard reality was the undeniable evidence that He had honored our trust in Him through all of these trouble-filled times. All was well. Again He had triumphed. I was glad, glad, glad. Life with Him surely was a thrill—an adventure!

This spiritual impetus surged through all of my being like a high-voltage electrical charge—not in the sense of an emotional high but in a much deeper dimension of perceiving the omnipotent power of Christ to accomplish such amazing achievements for those who truly trusted Him in trouble. No wonder He declares to us so clearly and categorically:

> "Trust in God."
> "All things are possible to him that believeth."
> "The just shall live by faith."

And, those of us who do, are not ashamed to declare in turn His utter faithfulness to us. For me, my trip to the rescue mission rekindled a flame of faith in Him for all of life's exigencies.

After this event, Ursula and I both began to feel sturdy enough to attend Sunday services on our own. Up until this time our friends were kind enough to call on us and take us to their churches. Some were very large and active congregations. Now at long last it was possible for us to revisit some of the smaller struggling places where we had poured out our time, our energy, our strength, our prayers, our tears, our teaching, and our love in days long ago.

When we had previously lived in Santa Barbara, it had been a source of deep concern to me that so many of its people were indifferent to God's Word and to Christ's claims upon them. I taught Bible studies all over the town, wherever anyone gave me a chance—in private homes, in business locations, at posh clubs, in large churches, and at small struggling churches. Because of my forthright and fearless delivery I was dubbed "the prophet"—but I came in compassion for a perishing community.

Now, once more, I was keen to find out what gracious work our Father had accomplished in some of these places. Little did I dream of what Christ had achieved. As with the rescue mission it would be a startling surprise and glorious thrill.

The very first little church we drove to was one where we had hoped God would work in an unusual way when we lived in the community. It was actually one of the oldest congregations, having been started in this little village of Goleta where we were staying.

Over the years, the handful of souls had acquired a choice location on a large piece of land to build a new sanctuary. All the facilities were in place, with ample accommodation for a Christian school. Most importantly, it was strategically situated close to the University of Santa Barbara with its very large student body. But much to my dismay, the work there seemed to stand still even though we had poured ourselves into the place and into its people.

In my moments of solitude and communion with Christ, I wondered sometimes if ever we would live long enough to see much fruit from that fellowship. We had done our best to be faithful. Now we could only wait on God's good time.

We now found that out waiting was at an end. The time of harvest had come. I knew this the instant we turned into the large parking lot. The whole area was packed solid with cars. People, young people, were pouring into the sanctuary. The same, dear, sweet, old stalwarts greeted us at the door with hugs, grins, and joyous faces. They did not need to say more.

All around us men were carrying in extra chairs until no more were to be found. The keen, enthusiastic pastor pled with people to sit closer so others could come in for worship.

My soul leaped with absolute exaltation and thanksgiving.

About eighty percent of the congregation were energetic, keen young couples and university students. My hope for this church had come alive!

I shall never, never forget the powerful, poignant message that the young pastor delivered from the Lord to his people that day. It was, without apology, simply this: We can declare to anyone that Jesus Christ is God, very God! It moved me mightily. I still read and reread the notes I made that morning.

That Sunday service was truly a tremendous thrill—another of Christ's amazing triumphs against trouble all these years. He had established a great victory in that place in His own time and in His own way.

Later that week, during a quiet conversation with the pastor, he explained that this church was even offering students a chance to earn credits in theology by taking special courses at the church. Marvelous, marvelous! He was on fire for the Most High in reaching out to this community.

As we were parting, he made a simple comment that touched me almost to tears. "Phillip, when we considered God's call to come here, it was the funding you provided that assured us we could reach this community for Christ." Now our Father had brought it all about. At long last His commitment to us had been carried out.

> He that goeth forth and weepeth, bearing precious seed, shall doubtless come again with rejoicing, bringing his sheaves with him (Ps. 126:6).

That is exactly what was happening, thrill upon thrill!

After that, Ursula and I made it a special point to attend an assortment of what used to be small, struggling, sparse little congregations. I was absolutely and hilariously astonished. Church after church was crammed full of people. Place after place had a new, eager, young pastor full of zeal, energy, and enthusiasm from on high. It was no wonder that our Father had brought us back once more to this lovely setting by the sea—not only just to renew my health to serve Him but also to see and hear and exult first hand in His gracious goodness to all of us.

On the wall of the tiny bedroom next to my office there hangs an aging calendar that we never tossed away. On one of its pages these stirring sentences are inscribed:

My Faithfulness

> I am the faithful God. I do not change, you can trust Me completely. Look to Me, lean on Me, and rest in Me.
>
> The words I have spoken are true, My promises are dependable, My covenants are reliable. All I have given you through My Son I have sealed forever with My holy vow.
>
> My faithfulness gives you confident hope, a sure foundation, and an anchor for your soul. I will never fail you.
>
> In faithfulness I keep what you have committed to Me, I perform My ministry through you, and perfect My love within you.
>
> I cared for you as a child. I will not forsake you as an adult (in old age).
>
> I have provided for you in times of need and I will care for you in the future.
>
> You will never be disappointed as you trust Me. You will never be put to shame.
>
> "Know therefore that the Lord thy God, He is God, the faithful God" (Deut. 7:9).
>
> —compiled by Roy Lessin

Every element of that magnificent declaration had been made real and viable in our times of trouble. Ultimately, unequivocally, it was my Father's faithfulness to us His children that made it possible to triumph.

Bless Him forevermore!

Chapter Fifteen

The Tide Turns

There is a pronounced ebb and flow to the events of life. This is especially true for the child of God who relies steadfastly on the Most High to bring him or her out of the offshore currents into a safe haven. There does come a change in circumstances and events that makes it clear that the tide is turning.

Part of this process, of course, lies with us. It is a matter of looking earnestly for the Father's hand in all of our affairs. It is a question of seeking and searching for any sign of His intervention on our behalf amid our adversity. It is for us to decide deep within that with His help we shall be on the alert to look for the bits of blue sky that break through the overcast.

In the preceding chapter, I recounted some stirring, spiritual, supernatural interludes. They were a tremendous impetus in arousing new hope and a sense of divine direction in all that touched us. We need that in life in order to be made whole. Truly, truly Christ was accomplishing that in a grand way!

But I was still locked in a battle with an elusive illness that seemed to relent, then return with the fury of an implacable foe. Some days I would feel fine, fit enough for long hikes on the beach, only to be laid flat again with a raging fever and a great weakness.

Fortunately we did not have a clinical thermometer with us. Nor did Ursula press the point of getting one. She would have been very alarmed if she had known what a furious fever was raging in my body. I would just lie on the couch, sleep as much as I could, and trust my Father to take me through the storm.

All of this slow, slow convalescence was compounded by complications with my teeth. Peculiar pains, very difficult to describe, began to shoot through my jaws, face, and head. I could not even be sure which tooth was causing the trouble. Eventually, under the expert care of our former dentist, the trouble was traced to its source. I prefer not to relive the agony endured to put things right to my tough, old teeth.

As Cheri would sometimes remark to me in her cute but compassionate way, "That's all you need. Just more trouble!" Her brown eyes would be warm and brimming with concern as she pronounced that last word with her special roll to every syllable. We had experienced it in double doses, but still we sensed that a shift was under way, and we would win in the end.

What encouraged me mightily was that the good days were beginning to outweigh the bad days. I was gaining ground. There were happy interludes with our friends when I could participate freely in the stream of social interaction that enables a person to love and be loved again as a whole person—not just a patient. One of these evenings lingers on in my memory with a peculiar potency. Somehow it bears a fragrance of pure pleasure like a rare perfume not forgotten. Let me quietly share its rare delight with you.

The young family who had brought the firewood to our door invited us to come over and have a part in the dad's birthday. They lived clear across the valley in a chaletlike home nestled in the high hills. In loving kindness they offered to fetch us for the festivities and take us home later that night.

As we drove across town the wee lad snuggled up to Ursula (Grandma) and the little lass cuddled up to me (Grandpa). It was a spontaneous, warm, tender gesture that made us glad. We knew without words that they had adopted us freely into their family.

At the house, a glorious fire burned hot. The logs of live oak and old avocado wood glowed red like chunks of coal. I settled myself on the great stone hearth, a happy youngster pushing in close on either side of me. In a matter of moments I was telling wild stories of bear, coyotes, deer, lions, and elephants. How they loved it! Questions tumbled from them. There were gales of laughter. Then, unable to contain themselves they would break away and race around the room in ecstasy.

It was as if I had been taken back in time thirty years—back to the days when in the prime of life I had roamed the mountains and plains, living under open skies. The days of my strength came back in joyous recollection. And in their glad reliving there was great newness of life.

At last we sat down to a delicious dinner prepared in love and joy. This time the wee lad sat beside me and his sweet sister near Grandma.

I was in for a special surprise. That tiny tot had already absorbed so much of the servant spirit from all of his family that he carefully tended to my every need. If it was another glass of water, he would get it. If it was another serving of vegetables, he would pass the dish. If it was the salt shaker, he handed it to me. It was a meal to remember. This was family dining at its best, sweetened with the pure delight of a little boy's spirit of service.

After the meal, when his dad and I went outdoors to fetch more wood for the fire, the wee fellow stood guard at the door. Every time one of us went in or out, loaded with wood, he would open and close the door to make the job that much easier.

Oh what a change there would be in our mad world if there were fifty million families who lived like that. When the tots were tucked in for the night, we sat in the gentle glow of the fire, expressing to these precious people our gratitude for their gracious generosity to us. Our visit was much more than just a joyous, happy celebration. A family had opened their hands, their home, and their hearts to take us into their lives. This is love at the bedrock level of human affection, human acceptance, and human approval. But beyond all of that, our fellowship was a simple yet sublime outpouring of our Father's love into our lives through theirs. Not only did they enfold us so warmly in their own winsome way, but in surrounding us with untarnished tenderness, they were Christ's angels helping us to triumph over our troubles. That night my soul was set to singing in contentment and well being.

Yes, indeed, the tide was turning.

In every area of activity, strength was returning.

After the long succession of trials, we were winning.

Whenever the days were drenched with sunlight after a winter storm I would head for the beach in search of driftwood. Streams, dry much of the year, would turn into rushing torrents of floodwater bearing along all sorts of trees, sticks, wood, and debris to the sea. A slender line of assorted logs, limbs, and broken wood littered the shore—free fireplace fuel to be carried home in glee. I was thrilled with this bonanza. Day by day I added to my woodpile on the patio, letting wind and sun and time dry it out for burning.

The physical exercise of searching the tide line and carrying the treasured chunks of wood seemed to be a marvelous therapy. There was purpose, direction, and practical benefit in the task. But some of my well-intentioned friends felt that it was a bit of folly. "Phillip, you have lost so much weight—you need to gain back at least fifteen pounds—yet you work it off."

I just smiled and kept on stacking the wood. At the same time, my appetite, which even at normal times is remarkable, began to gather momentum. At meals, I would consume mountains of food, which astounded even Cheri who loves to see me eat. She insists that my hearty appetite is one of the greatest rewards for her fine cooking. I have always felt that my keen appetite is a unique and special benefit from above. I just relish vegetables, fruit, dairy products, and mountains of meat—all kinds, prepared any way.

Despite consuming such generous quantities of food my weight had scarcely varied more than two pounds either way for years and years. It stood at 168 pounds almost as if locked between 166 and 170 pounds. But here I was down to about 153 pounds and I could not seem to come back.

One night, in a serious frame of mind, Ursula said that she was beginning to agree with our friends that I simply had to slow down my stern regime of exercise in my struggle to regain strength. "You hike for miles. You swim diligently every day. You pack wood. It's time you ease off a bit."

Then a startling incident brought the wood gathering to a sudden stop. It was a warm morning after a real southwester. Chunks of wood were everywhere. And I was busy as a beaver carrying it away. I was carrying two large chunks but dropped them on the sand to rest and chat with a small lad and his dad who were building sand castles.

The boy's father looked at me as if I was a bit unhinged. "What you doing with that wood?" he grunted peevishly.

"Taking it home for the fireplace," I replied with a grin.

"You're nuts, man. Absolutely nuts!" He meant it.

"Why do you say that?" I asked a bit bewildered.

"Can't you see its coated with contaminants?" He pointed out spots on the bark and broken fibers that were saturated with pesticides, old oil deposits, and other pollutants. "Don't you know the state has a ban on burning beach wood because it is so dangerous?" He was almost angry now—obviously I was a dodo.

"I'm just a visitor here from the north," I added.

"Well," his face softened a shade, "if you have been burning this junk in your fireplace I'm surprised you aren't dead." With that he went back to building sand castles.

I thanked him heartily and headed home empty-handed. Clearly, clearly I recalled the nights that I had huddled up to my open fires, inhaling their fumes and fragrance, marveling at the multicolored flames, wondering what caused the varied hues, even drawing close enough to the radiant heat to spend a sleepless night in its embrace.

Was this part of the perverse problem with my health?

Was this why I became ill again and again?

Was this another key to turn the lock on my life?

I accepted the stranger on the sun-splashed beach as another of my Father's gentle angels in disguise.

All my precious pile of wood had to go. I began the reverse job of dragging it all back. No one dared be allowed to burn this dangerous driftwood. It was wearisome work until only one large, last load remained. I had tossed it all out on the sidewalk, prepared to pack it the long, long distance back to the car.

Just then a Hispanic gardener came along. "What nice, nice wood," he exclaimed. "Beautiful, Beautiful!"

In response, I warned him of its dangers.

"Oh, no, no burn!" He smiled. "I will take it all to decorate the rockery in my garden." In short order he bore it all away in glee. And again, my Father had sent His special servant to help turn the tide.

From that time on my health began to improve swiftly. My weight started to return steadily but surely. It was almost like dawn beginning to break over the eastern skyline after a long, dark, difficult night.

Friends invited us to share picnics beside the sea, up in the hills, or at any spot where the California spring was breaking into abundant life after the long winter of trouble. Both outside and inside Christ was working His wonders for us, and I was glad, glad, glad! I was humble in spirit because of all His mercy and jubilant in soul because of buoyed renewal.

One sunny day, our closest friends invited us to share a huge, freshly baked pepperoni pizza on the beach. This was a first for me, but I was game for anything. Piping hot in temperature and in taste, I ate the pizza with relish, standing out in the breakers with waves washing up around my suntanned legs. That must be pretty close to paradise!

That night the refrain of my spirit repeated over and over in my heart.

> Bless the LORD, O my soul: and all that is within me, bless his holy name. Bless the LORD, O my soul, and forget not all his benefits: Who forgiveth all thine iniquities; who healeth all thy diseases (Ps. 103:1–3).

Chapter Sixteen

California Quake

What I [the Lord your God] want from you is your true thanks; I want your promises fulfilled. I want you to trust me in your times of trouble, so I can rescue you, and you can give me glory (Ps. 50:14–15 TLB).

To live out the words of this verse is to look hard for fragments of loveliness in the most ordinary events of life. It is to search and seek and seize evidence of the beautiful bonuses bestowed by the gentle hands of our loving Father. Day by day, as strength returned, I would very deliberately be thankful—sometimes for the great, glorious clouds rolling across the ocean and over the mountains to the north, and at other times for the fresh fragrance of flowers, earth, and trees after a rain.

With an acute and remarkable awareness there had been an ever-increasing inner assurance that our Father was very much with us in all our difficulties. Like little children, we were reassured that all was well. We were having our faith fortified, which was wonderful beyond words, for we live in a most fragile and uncertain society. The world of California is one that can easily be shaken.

I have written and spoken much about this theme to my generation. Christ had given me stern warnings again and again to alert our people to their peril. Many in derision had dismissed me as something of an Old Testament prophet. No matter. The day draws near that unless our people turn and seek God's mercy and turn from their wicked ways, disaster will come. This is not to be negative. It is the positive cry of the hour.

Then, early one morning about 4:30 A.M., the hour at which I often begin the day, the whole world began to quake, to shake, and to sway. It reminded me in the first few seconds of rocking a child gently to and fro in an old-fashioned cradle.

But the momentum quickened. Lamps and lights began to sway and rattle. The room began to roll and heave. I awakened Ursula and we dove under a strong sturdy table with thick heavy legs. There we waited out the worst of the quake.

In the suite upstairs, a Swiss clock maker repaired huge grandfather clocks. One of the first thoughts that rushed through my mind was that they might crash through the floor like great, heavy missiles. But fortunately the damage did not go that far.

Then the lights went out. "There's been a massive power failure in the electrical distribution grid," I remarked to Cheri. "It may cover most of southern California." I was eerily correct.

Now there was total darkness.

A sinister silence settled in.

No lights, no usual radio broadcasts, and no TV.

No heat, no cooking, no warmth, and no energy.

Ursula recalled a tape player we had been loaned that also had a shortwave band. She groped for our one old flashlight, found the tape player, fiddled with the dials, and finally found a shortwave broadcast warning everyone.

- Don't light matches or candles, lest a broken gas line explodes.
- Don't light fires, lest your broken chimney burns up the house.
- Don't go out in traffic—highways are smashed. There are no signals for traffic.
- Don't drink your water. Boil it.

But how do you boil water with no energy, no power, no stove, and no fireplace? How do you get food? Only one supermarket with a standby generator would even open its doors to customers. Cheri found that place—and also had a cup of hot coffee there to warm her up a bit. It was all a ghastly replay of her girlhood days when she had gone through barbaric, bombing raids of World War II.

Then, too, there had been no light, no power, no food, and no sure shelter. She had survived then. She was sure we could survive again with calm determination and quiet trust in Christ.

While she was gone in search of another flashlight, a bit of food and some bottled water to drink, I went in search of gasoline for the Sonata. The tank was almost empty. In case of another massive shock, it might be necessary to head home.

There was a gas station, only a block from us. But it was shut down, empty of cars. The proprietor was inside. He simply shrugged his shoulders, waved two empty hands at me, and said, "No power to pump gas. All the computers are down. Only two stations in this whole area have generators."

Little by little it became painfully apparent that with all of the so-called preparations made for a quake, there really was no adequate safety net. Modern man with all his scientific skills and his pompous pride in modern technology could not preserve himself from such a peril.

There was death. There was dislocation. There was enormous damage. This quake was declared to be the greatest natural disaster to ever strike the United States of America.

For me it was God's wake-up call to a people who resented Christ's gospel.

People we met, who loved California and had lived there all their lives, now decided to leave at once. Some were so terrified of even returning to their shaken, shattered homes that they were preparing to look for a home far to the east in some other state. It was a time of enormous soul-searching. Were they ready for the "big one" yet to come? Seismologists predicted it could have a shattering force two hundred times more destructive.

Yes, we lived in dangerous days.

What would it yet take to awaken people?

Perhaps this disaster would make modern humanity realize how utterly vulnerable they are.

Or will their persistent pride still flaunt itself?

In the midst of all this chaos and confusion there was a knock at our door. No, not even a doorbell could ring. In amazement I wondered who it might be. There stood a friend who lived only a few blocks from us. He had on huge winter boots, heavy winter clothing, and thick mitts.

"When the power went out, I thought of you people at once, in this all-electric suite. I knew you would need wood for the fireplace. I've brought you a whole truck load from my place."

What a selfless soul!

It took a bit of time to believe it could be true.

In the crucible of a crisis like this he cared that much about a neighbor.

Such a generous gesture of goodwill stirred my spirit. By the time Ursula got back with her bottle of water, some matches, and a flashlight, the patio was piled full of fuel wood from our friend.

To the reader who may live in parts of the country where firewood is plentiful, this episode may seem a small thing. In the place where we stayed, wood was not sold by the cord. It was sold in small prepackaged bundles in the stores, each one costing about three dollars for five or six sticks. It was expensive fuel indeed.

But that was not the point.

The sheer generosity of a friend in our hour of adversity was what counted. It was a royal reminder that amidst disaster there are people who display the wondrous love of Christ with calm action and quiet concern.

Is it not remarkable that out of all the events of that unforgettable earthquake this simple, sincere servant spirit should stand out in my memory as a symbol of hope, light, and good cheer? Our shaky world needs that sort of attitude if it is to survive and flourish in the face of great trouble.

Shortly after this, Ursula and I were eager to go over and visit a friend whose husband had died a few weeks after our arrival. I had been so ill that it had simply been impossible to attend his funeral.

When we called to see when it would be convenient to come,

she was eager to see us. So we set a date and arrived in due course wondering just how she would handle this great loss in her life.

Cancer had done its dreadful work. There had been such a long and bruising battle to beat it, yet, in the end it had claimed her lifelong companion. Now she was alone. The earthquake had come. What dreadful disaster would be next?

As soon as we entered the sun-splashed living room of her home I sensed the magnificent serenity of this woman's spirit. The palpable presence of the living Christ was everywhere apparent. Her gentle demeanor, her calm assurance, her quiet strength all came from Christ.

We Christians speak much about such a spirit.

When we encounter it in real life we are amazed.

It is the immanence of Christ among us.

She recounted to us in remarkable detail all the long struggle they had faced in the battle with that dread disease. Not once was there a hint of self-pity for herself in the midst of so much suffering. Finally, the strong warrior was laid to rest. She was at peace. All was well.

Softly she moved around the room, serving us tea and biscuits. It was as if we were being waited upon by an angel in human guise. Here was unusual grace and strength of divine proportions.

I asked if she had any apprehension about living alone now. She replied openly, frankly, and honestly without pretense. "None at all! I have no fear. He, my Lord, is always here." A gentle, glorious smile lit up her face in joyous radiance. Even the earthquake had not alarmed her. She was glad that her spouse had "missed the big one." Who knew how many more after shocks and terrifying tremors there would be?

When we parted, I knew that our Father had made this a sacred hour. In an unusual way, we had heard Christ say again,

> In this world ye shall have tribulation: but be of good cheer; I have overcome the world (John 16:33).

As we drove home through the fading, golden light it was as if the entire earth radiated a supernatural splendor. The foliage of trees, shrubs, and flowers pulsed with pure light.

The sky glowed with the setting sun sinking beyond the rim of the Pacific. It was an interlude of profound peace. In the midst of death, disaster, and what might have been despair, He spoke to us once more, as of old,

> I am the resurrection, and the life: he that believeth in me, though he were dead, yet shall he live (John 11:25).

Both Ursula and I had been touched at great, deep profound levels of life on this day. We could barely speak above a whisper. It was as if, in truth, we were traveling in company with the living Christ. And really, we were.

From that interlude an unshakable assurance swept through my spirit that we could triumph against any trouble of any sort no matter how severe. The living Lord God who had declared to Moses at the burning bush, "I AM hath sent me unto you" (Ex. 3:14) was saying the same to us.

> I am the one who brought you here.
> I am the one who cared for you.
> I am the one who will take you on.
> I am your refuge, your strength.
> I am your deliverer from disease.
> I am your protection in peril.
> I am your provider.

New life, renewed energy, increasing faith, and joyous hope all sprang anew within my soul. Our Father, in His intimate knowledge of my need, had reached out His great hand of love and encouragement to us through this winsome widow. No wonder Christ cared so tenderly for widows.

Chapter Seventeen

Heading Home

As my health improved, so too did the days seem to speed by in rapid succession. The time to return home to Canada was looming larger in my thoughts: *Would there be sufficient strength for the long haul home?* We faced a long mid-winter drive of over thirteen hundred miles through our western mountains.

I kept reassuring Ursula that I was sure I was up to the challenge. The weather reports were not always that promising as the final few days went by. Still, I was confident that there would be a break in between storm systems. Then with the dear old Sonata set free to "fly" we would be home in short order.

During our last week in the south I was asked to lead a study session with a group of university people who met in a private home. One of them came to pick me up and offered to take me back when the session was over. I appreciated this kindness.

My theme, given to me by Christ for that evening was: "The Challenge to Live for Christ on Campus." It was remarkable how keen the young men and women really were. They were intent on asking searching, serious questions. Most importantly the gracious Spirit of God had spoken emphatically to some of those who were more mature.

It has always been a spiritual stimulus for me to see young people prepared to follow Christ at great personal cost. These are the brave, bold leaders of tomorrow who pick up the flame of faith in Christ and live for Him without apology.

One splendid young man gripped my hand hard. With blazing eyes he declared, "Beginning tomorrow, I shall live only for Him."

Just to spend the evening with this study group had done my spirit great good. Yes, our Father was very much at work on the campus of the nearby university. He was calling our choice, brilliant young people from that place to accomplish great and stirring exploits. It had been worth a winter of testing to see this happening—another of the truly beautiful bonuses bestowed by our loving Father.

As the last few days swept by, we were happily blessed with warm temperatures and long hours of winter sun. Some storms had swept through a few days before, dressing the mountain ranges to the north in sparkling snow, but it soon melted in the sun. I spent my time on long tramps along the tide line.

These quiet times by the ocean edge have always been precious interludes for me. There is more than just magnificent scenery. There are times of intense, intimate interaction with Christ my Friend. There are times of utter stillness to allow Him to speak to my spirit at profound depths and in compelling ways. There are times to give my Father unabashed praise, thanks, and genuine gratitude.

It was on that splendid strand of sand and cliffs and surging surf that He assured me again that there was still much service to perform for Him and His people. I was to head home—restored, renewed, and made whole—to write more books, to teach more classes, to touch more lives, and to show His strength to my generation. He would take my hand and help in every endeavor.

I shall never, ever, forget the last hour I spent on that beach. I stood on a rocky headland jutting out into the thundering surf. The breaking waves rushed into all the little coves around me. Every bit of broken flotsam and jetsam was swept away by the swirling waters. The rocks, the sand, and the cliffs all glistened clean and shining in the sun. It was indeed a brand-new day, a brand-new beginning for this bit of beach, cleansed and renewed by the power of the incoming tide.

For me, too, as I stood straight and tall and strong on that great rock it was a brand-new day, a brand-new beginning in God's great hand. Wherever He led me, and whatever He asked, I was ready and eager to go. The weary winter was over. The time of trouble was past. The hour of triumph in His might had come.

I turned and walked away in quiet contentment.

As always, my Father had been faithful to me.

I was ready for the road.

In an hour we would be away.

Kind, kind friends came to bid us good-bye as we shut up the little suite and closed its door for the last time. Surely, surely that had been a tough trysting place. But it had also been the place of Christ's arrangement where He enabled us to triumph against trouble.

Our friends hugged us hard—not with halfway hugs but with hearty hugs, big bear hugs, and honorable hugs that spoke worlds of affection, esteem, and sweet consolation. They promised that the next time they would make the long trip north to see us.

We parted in peace. I swung the Sonata out onto the freeway. In minutes we were soaring up the coast. The car felt like it wanted to fly.

Another kind friend, living in Santa Maria, some seventy miles to the northwest of Santa Barbara, had invited us to spend the first evening in her home. I had accepted this offer gladly, for up to this day I had never driven more than thirty-five miles at a single stretch without excruciating pains. So, driving seventy miles the first day would double the distance and show how well I could handle the car. To my unbounded surprise, I did not seem to have any difficulty. The pain was virtually absent. My hopes soared, and we went to bed confident that we could get home in a hurry.

In the past, this dear woman and her hearty husband had thrown open their home for me to hold Bible studies there. Week after week I would drive the seventy miles up and back to Santa Barbara to teach the eager people who came. I remembered vividly the late-night drives home when dense fog swept in from the ocean and draped the hills in clinging veils of whiteness. I would get home weary, with bloodshot eyes from staring into the gloom. I wondered about the next morning.

Meanwhile we gave thanks for this dear lady who, after her husband had suddenly been called home, with God's grace had started a new chapter in her life. She was buoyant, bright, and filled with fresh hope for the years ahead.

We left the next day at dawn. Sure enough, within half an hour we were enfolded in dense fog. But it did not last. As the sun came over the Sierras to the east the fog burned away, and we burned up the highway. I felt excellent. The Sonata cruised effortlessly at a steady 65 mph. Ursula, all smiles remarked in her jaunty, happy, way, "When angels travel, the sky always smiles." It was a cute saying that she had carried over with her from childhood years.

She had prepared us delicious sandwiches. Every couple of hours we would pull off on a side road, stretch our legs, munch a sandwich, and let the sweet running engine cool down. To my great joy there was virtually no pain or discomfort in driving. It really was a miracle. Ursula was astounded that we could keep up such a pace hour after hour. We were making remarkable time. "Thank you, Father!" I had driven twelve hours without tiring.

We swept up and over the giant foothills of Mount Shasta. The mighty mountain was utterly magnificent under a heavy mantle of new snow that shone in the sun. I shot some glorious pictures of its breathtaking beauty. What a day! I could hardly believe that we were covering the ground so rapidly. Still I had no pain, no discomfort, and no strain. By dusk we would be well into Oregon and halfway home.

We found a quiet motel, had a hot dinner and a hot bath in short order. I slept like a log. At 4:30 A.M. we were on the road again. The skies were clear, the stars sharp, clear, and silver bright.

Then suddenly, swiftly everything changed. We were climbing into high country. Snow began to fall menacingly. It was covering the road quickly. Visibility diminished to almost zero. All the yellow lines were obliterated. We were driving in blizzard conditions in a virtual whiteout. The road surface was a glare of ice.

Could we go on?

Should we pull off on a side road and sit it out?

I lifted my soul in silent petition. *Father, kindly guide us!*

Just then a huge, fully loaded logging truck pulled out onto the highway in front of us. He had a mighty mountain of ponderosa pine logs chained on his outfit. But most importantly he had a remarkable bank of brilliant red lights all across the back of his load. I could see where he went as clear as could be. He was obviously a local logger who knew every inch of the road.

Here he was, now, breaking trail for us through the deepening snow. He was leading us surely, safely through the storm, simply beckoning us mile after mile: *Follow me!* Quietly I remarked to Ursula, "I never dreamed I would ever live to see the day our father would send us a rough, tough logger as His angel in disguise!" But He had. That truck guided us through that blizzard in a whiteout before the break of day in absolute safety.

At long last, the storm passed. Dawn came and we pulled into a tiny two-bit cafe. I was one ravenous man. The huge breakfast of steak, eggs, hash browns, toast, jelly, and coffee would keep me going until we got home.

Carefully we chose our route through low country. Snow draped all the northern ranges. I refused to fight my way over any more high passes. We would drive quickly along the river valleys. It would be a long, long day.

Furious winds funneled down into the deep valleys from the north. Even the heavily loaded Sonata with its low, smooth profile was pounded and buffeted about. Still we pushed on. We were headed home. There was no stopping us.

A huge golden cock pheasant exploded out of the brush beside the road. In a flash of feathers, the beautiful big bird was blasted into our windshield by the wind. There was a terrible crash. I ducked down, expecting the glass to shatter full in my face. It did not even crack! As for the beleaguered bird, the wind must have carried him clear off into the bush, for we never saw him again.

Just at dusk, as the sun set behind the hills across our lovely lake, I turned the tired Sonata into our drive. We had been traveling relentlessly for fourteen hours in mid-winter weather. We were home again—safe and snug and overflowing with gratitude and quiet contentment.

The house on the hill was warm and inviting. Dear neighbors had put on the heat for us. The wanderers were home—home from the hills and far-away places—home to rest and relax in familiar surroundings and to relish our own beds and rooms and quiet country atmosphere.

But then the phone rang!

We had been home less than twenty minutes.

It was a long-distance call regarding my teaching classes.

We could scarcely believe how soon the action came.

Obviously what had been made so clear to me in Santa Barbara was leaping into life up here. In fact, day upon day, week upon week, calls came in to take services, speak at retreats, conduct classes here and there and everywhere. It would be a full, full year.

Then there were books to write, several were clearly impressed upon my spirit. Work on this one began within three days. Once again I was strong and fit and free of pain. The long time of trouble was behind us. A new, bright, abundant chapter of service had started. Bless His name!

It is Christ who empowers us to triumph.

Chapter Eighteen

The Stirring of Spring

Spring came with a compulsion, an insistence, a sure change that was unique. The days pulsed with powerful sunlight that quickly warmed the whole world. Frequently, the nights were bathed in gentle, soft showers. Green grass sprang from the earth with astonishing vigor. Buds burst open in green glory from shrubs and trees. Flowers unfurled in the warm winds like flags flying. There was change, color, and vibrant action in the earth around us.

I could not recall when the spring season had stirred me so deeply—not just because of the wondrous beauty of the earth but also because of a profound inner conviction that Ursula and I were on the very edge of great changes in our adventuresome walk with our Father. It was as if the warm wind of His own gracious Spirit was moving gently upon our spirits. The profound impression persisted within that we were to face great, new challenges in the months to come. They would not be easy but in them, Christ would again enable us to triumph in His might.

The very first of these came in physical form. Although both of us had recovered in a remarkable way from the severe illnesses that we had endured that winter, it was apparent that our strength and stamina had been diminished. I soon realized that it was imperative to install an automatic sprinkler system to water the grounds. The strength to haul hoses around in the heat, to change sprinklers day and night, and to keep track of the endless time changes was no longer available.

It was fortunate indeed that this acute awareness came to me so early in the season. In short order an excellent underground system was installed just in time, for the hottest year ever experienced in this already sun-drenched valley was upon us. Our Father knew what lay ahead of us. In His gentle way He had prepared us for it. I came to love the sound of the sprinklers refreshing the grounds at the break of day. Great gratitude welled up within. This way we could beat the heat!

Much the same sort of stern challenge faced Cheri. She has always been a meticulous homemaker. But this year spring cleaning seemed beyond her. The numerous large glass doors that were such a prominent part of our home would require a professional cleaner this year, and there were so many wide windows looking out over the lake and mountains that were more than her match now. Again, happily, and with a minimum of expense, we were able to engage an excellent window cleaner. In short order he had all the glass sparkling.

But our joy was to be rather short-lived. Soon we were to discover that her lack of energy was more, much more, than a carryover from her winter illness. It was soon determined that she had a serious bacterial infection in her eyes. This condition was further complicated by very high blood pressure, an excessive cholesterol count, plus the much aggravated possibility of a serious stroke.

To her great credit, she set her will like steel to get well. She embarked on a rigid regime of putting warm compresses on her eyes then bathing them in chamomile tea. She cut out all her beloved sweets, candies, chocolates, and cookies with astonishing courage. I was amazed!

Every deliberate action that she undertook we also undergirded with earnest prayer and the sincere request that Christ would empower her to stay with her spartan lifestyle. To put it plainly, the results were remarkable. Even the eye specialist was delighted with her rapid recovery.

In a matter of weeks, the infection in her eyes had well nigh disappeared. Her blood pressure steadily diminished until it was normal. Her high cholesterol count was reduced. She lost weight gradually, thrilled to regain her slim, trim figure. And, perhaps most importantly, her energy level began to increase once more as she slept better.

Both of us were elated and so thankful for her turnaround. Still, at our age it was clear that the time was approaching when we needed to consider moving to a smaller home that took less care, less strength, and less time to maintain. This is always a formidable decision in life. We are not wise enough, even at the best of times, to know exactly when to move, where to go next, or how to do it. So many seniors make serious mistakes at this point. I was determined not to depend on human expertise. Our Father was the One to determine what was best for us as His children.

Finally, on a hot, mid-June afternoon, I felt compelled by God's Spirit to seek His divine guidance. At such moments I am but a child, coming to my Father in calm confidence that He will hear my simple petition.

Quiet and alone, I bowed my head in reverence over my desk. Then I made this profound plea, "My Father, Only You know the future. Only You can comprehend our needs in this hour of decision. Only You know what is best for us.

"This is Your home. You entrusted us with its care. If Your time has come for us to move, I trust You to send us the buyers of Your choice. Then we will know Your will.

"I do not wish to run ahead of you. I will not put up a For Sale sign or even engage an agent. I trust only You.

"When You send the buyers to our door, we will know that Your time has come for us to move. Thank you, Father!"

That is all that was spoken in calm faith. I lifted my head and sensed the presence of Christ pervading the whole office. In peace, I stood. All was well. He was here. I went out in power, His power.

It was the very next day, Tuesday, at noon that the telephone rang while we were eating lunch. The voice on the other end was familiar. It was my friend Frank, the agent who had sold me this house five-and-a-half years before.

He is a good-natured fellow who loves to tease me. "Phillip," he chuckled, "you have been in that house long enough. Time for you to move. I have clients from Germany looking for property just like yours. Can I bring them to see your home this afternoon?"

Carefully I explained to him that I had asked our Father, just the day before, to send us buyers when it was His time for us to move. Little did I know it would be this sudden.

So, in great glee we arranged to meet, arrive at a proper price for the property, lay out the commission arrangements, and establish the date of occupancy. The latter was important, first because I had Bible studies for the summer, an absolute priority, and second because we had no clear idea where our Father would lead us next. We did not wish to be hasty.

It was agreed that the clients could come the next morning to view the property. By then we would have the house in first-class order for them to see.

Ursula had a morning engagement in town, so I was alone when the visitors arrived. They were highly excited, chattering away in German when I opened the door. They burst into the lovely front room with its heart-stopping, panoramic views over the valley and lake. They stood astonished.

"It's beautiful! It's beautiful!" They exclaimed aloud. I agreed heartily.

"Yes, yes! We think it is beautiful, too, a lovely place to live!"

It was enough. That afternoon the deal was done. We were to be paid our price in full, all cash, when their funds were transferred from banks in Switzerland. What was more, we were given full use of the home until all my teaching responsibilities were discharged.

What a swift, smooth, satisfying sort of transaction. Once more our loving Lord had arranged our affairs in wondrous ways. We bowed before Him in humility, gratitude, awe, and wonder.

Because the excited purchasers had rushed around the grounds snapping pictures of "their place," I had to break the news gently to our neighbors. It seemed to them unbelievable that a house could be sold so quickly without even putting up a For Sale sign. So much fun!

Chapter Nineteen

Fire Season

Following a luxuriant spring, little did we dream what a time of trouble the summer would be for our mountain valley. Ursula and I were by no means alone in this. It would turn out to be a traumatic test of endurance, hardship, and suffering for thousands of people.

The first signs that we were in for a formidable forest-fire season were the high daytime temperatures. Even in ordinary years July and August are hot in this semidesert country. But this summer our hills and rocks pulsed and panted with heat under the searing sun.

Again and again, I gave sincere and hearty thanks for the efficient underground sprinklers. But even then it seemed that some trees, shrubs, and plants would succumb without extra water. Besides this, I had planted new trees and a beautiful vegetable garden that demanded more attention than usual. Now that the house was sold, I felt doubly responsible to keep the place in excellent order for the new owners.

On top of this we had begun to do the essential sorting and packing that is called for in any move. For us, this was unusually challenging for two reasons. First, we were determined that the time had come to downscale into a smaller home. Second, we felt that it was the opportunity to dispose of everything not essentially useful. Not knowing precisely where our Father would lead us next, nor to what service He might assign us, this was not an easy process. There were scores and scores of difficult decisions to make, some of them painful choices. What should go? What would remain?

All my life I have been a man on the move. For this reason my belongings have been kept down to an absolute minimum, ready to be packed on short notice and transported with swift dispatch. Still the oppressive heat made all the sorting a tough task. By day's end both of us were just about ready to drop.

Sometimes we wondered if we could face another file, work through another shelf of books, or pack another carton of household effects. Once or twice I teased Cheri with the comment, "A fire would soon fix it all."

Then, suddenly, one day a huge, ominous, dark plume of smoke began to rise behind the rugged hills just north of us. I knew at once that a gigantic forest fire had ignited in the timber and tinder-dry, rocky terrain east of our town some eight miles away. What followed was a furious battle to try and preserve the people and their homes from destruction. Because of the rocky terrain, high winds, and unusually dry underbrush the fire spread with terrifying intensity.

Homes in the hills were burned to heaps of smoldering ruins and gray ashes. Hundreds, then thousands of fire-threatened residents were evacuated. The whole area was put on fire alert. Huge water bombers, helicopters, bulldozers, and squads of firefighters were called to combat the inferno.

Day after day, the gigantic water bombers roared and thundered over our home. They were picking up tons of water from the lake in front of us, so we had a firsthand, ringside view of their daring runs. Sometimes I wondered if the monsters would tear the tiles off our roof as they labored to gain altitude.

We, too, were served notice to stand ready for early evacuation if the fire spread into our area. The air was heavy with smoke. Soot and ash and burned debris settled out of the sky. The sun glowed red through the evening overcast. The moon was a dull orange in the night sky. I stood in the darkness, hose in hand, wetting down all the vegetation around the house, asking our Father to preserve us all from this great peril.

As it turned out not a single life was lost in the forest fire, but the destruction to property was great. The cost of containing the fire that consumed thousands of acres ran into the millions of dollars. The bright side was the generous spirit of goodwill and concern shown by so many people in this hour of danger.

The fire was so widespread that it drove wildlife out of the hills to seek food and refuge in the orchards and gardens of landowners below. We had our share of nighttime visitors. Deer, skunks, and especially coons came in search of fruit, vegetables, and other green tasty morsels. To my amazement, they tore up the garden as if a bulldozer had been there. It was all part of the hot, hot summer that called for extra work and effort to keep things right.

Fortunately for us, the garden produced such an astonishing abundance of fruit and vegetables that there was ample for all of us. Not only could our wild visitors enjoy the bounty but also our neighbors and friends. I carried bowls of beans, tomatoes, lettuce, peas, apricots, and other produce to all sorts of people. This was a special pleasure!

In the meantime, Cheri and I earnestly entreated our Father to guide us to our next home. At first we felt it might mean a return to California. New and encouraging opportunities to work among the university students were developing. But, so too, were the calls to serve young people and various groups right in this burgeoning valley. Only Christ, by His gracious Spirit could and would lead us to the place of His choice. Above all else we wished to do His bidding.

So, quietly and without fanfare we began to search for the place He had prepared for us. This was an act of faith. Constantly we asked to have our own spirits attuned and made very sensitive to His Spirit. We refused to insist on our own desires or wishes in choosing a new home. The place of peace—the location with deep contentment—would be where our Father wanted us to live. Finding it out was an adventure.

One afternoon, quite by chance, we came across a cute little home that was exactly suited to our needs. It sat amid a secluded cluster of homes high in the hills. There were graceful trees that surrounded it, so it appeared to be a place of peace.

Cheri and I asked to inspect the home several times. The more we looked at the property, the more it appealed to us. Finally, we decided to call our agent to come and draw up the proper papers for us the following day.

At dawn, however, during my quiet hour of communion with our Lord, a compelling, insistent, inner conviction came over my spirit that we should not proceed with the purchase. Somehow this would be a mistake. When Frank arrived around noon I suggested that we pray together and seek our Father's wisdom. Then I looked into my friend's sparkling eyes and asked if he knew of a single reason why we should not buy this home.

His reply was astonishing. "Phillip, I am glad you asked. This morning I just found out that the quiet road in front of that house is to be widened. All the trees are to be torn out. Heavy construction traffic will roar by the door. A major new development is planned just behind the house."

It was enough. At this crucial juncture our Father had spared us from making a drastic, wrong decision. In a gesture of profound appreciation and enormous relief, I raised my arms in a gesture of genuine gratitude to Christ for His counsel. Truly, truly He could be trusted! About ten days later a huge fire burned the main lodge in this same exclusive development to the ground. All in all we would have suffered enormous setbacks in that location. In His wondrous ways, our Father had preserved us. Our agent, now advised us he had some major commitments at the coast. He would be away for a spell, so we decided that our search would continue quietly on our own. Little did we imagine how quickly another, much more desirable place would be found. What excitement Christ can generate for those who joyfully follow Him in explicit, calm confidence.

Meanwhile Ursula, in her own remarkable perseverance was having good success in selling our surplus furniture. She amazed me to no end with her energetic enthusiasm. Her health was improving steadily, so, with skill and joy, she disposed of furnishings we would never need again—all the time dreaming of finding a few choice pieces to adorn any little place we might find suitable for her to nest in again.

Just the anticipation made her smile, smile, smile!

Chapter Twenty

The Fun of Finding a New Home

During this house search, another series of summer Bible studies had been started in the next town. Despite the oppressive heat and heavy traffic on the crowded roads, I was given the strength and stamina to carry out the heavy responsibility. It was astonishing that so many people, eager to be taught, turned out each week.

It was especially heartening to see the enthusiasm and earnestness of young people, willing and ready to respond to God's Word. For a man well advanced in years, it is wondrous joy to see the next generation prepared to give their best to God Himself. His Spirit moved among us with profound power, touching lives at great depths. It was well worth all the work to see young and old follow Christ.

Then, one day, amid all this activity, an inconspicuous little flyer was dropped in our mailbox. In one lower corner there was a short, simple advertisement for a cottage with waterfront. All that went with it was an agent's phone number and a price well below anything usually asked for this kind of property.

Our agent was away, so I called his wife, a newly licensed real-estate representative. Would she care to find out more about this place? She would—efficiently, urgently, and enthusiastically.

However, knowing us well, and our preference for a place in the country, she was not at all sure that this gated community just on the edge of town would suit us at all. Still she would be glad to show us the house. So we picked up Frank's wife, Jean, and set out on our search. Cheri and I had never, ever been into Redwing Resorts by the lake and river. It was a first-time view for us.

The moment I drove through the handsome gates, a compelling, but calm inner conviction swept into my spirit. The home of our hopes was here The lovely streets were bordered with beautiful landscaping. The trim, neat, sparkling cottages, the quietness and peace of the place, and the contented faces of the home owners spoke volumes.

Both Cheri and I were astonished. Although we had lived in this valley for years, we had no knowledge of this lovely location. It was as if suddenly a great wide door was thrown open before us and we were invited in for our first look. We were literal strangers to this special spot.

A cordial groundsman showed us into the handsome lodge built on the beach. We were taken aback with the gorgeous grounds and lush green lawns running down to the lake shore. Wild geese, white gulls, grebe, ducks, and herons relished the quiet waters above the dam where the lake spilled into the river. It was beautiful, beautiful!

I simply gasped in amazement. "I never knew there was such a gorgeous spot here. It is a bit like the beautiful Bouchart Gardens near Victoria. And today we have found it." Better to have said, "Today our Father has lead us here, to the special place of His appointment!"

The first cottage, the one advertised in the flyer, was a bit too small—too cramped to accommodate our needs. But just a few doors further down the river another sparkling home was for sale. At my urging, Jean gathered up her courage, knocked on the door, and asked the owner if we might take a peek. She was delighted to show us through. She had recently been widowed and wished to locate near her children in Calgary.

Cheri and I stood rather breathless in this home. Quality, skill, and enormous attention to detail had gone into its construction. It was almost like new, only three years old, kept in immaculate condition by this gracious, elegant, refined lady. She showed us everything. A gorgeous, bright sunroom overlooking the river and its cascading falls adorned the front of the home.

We stood awestruck in the center of the home. I whispered, "Honey, this is the home our Father has prepared for us."

Not a single shred of doubt remained in my mind.

The long search was over.

We were home!

Peace, such as only Christ can bestow.

Within hours an offer was made on the house. It was accepted at once. We were elated. Even more remarkably the owner called within the hour to tell us how much she appreciated the smooth transaction. She was a gracious lady.

From that day forward, Cheri and I resembled a couple of young newlyweds preparing to move into their first home. An electric excitement of pure pleasure and eager expectancy surged through our souls. It did not seem possible that people our age could realize so much joy and unabashed delight in such a simple move.

Truly, truly that glorious declaration of Christ's care for His people had come true in real life for us.

> Who satisfieth thy mouth with good things; so that thy youth is renewed like the eagle's (Ps. 103:5).

We were rejuvenated with irrepressible joy. We spoke continually of our next nest with jubilation.

Piece by piece, all the packing was completed with care and precision. What at the outset had seemed an insurmountable mountain of work was steadily but surely whittled down to manageable proportions. Day upon day we called upon Christ not only for the stamina needed but also for the astute wisdom to work with skill.

He responded in a remarkable manner to our petitions, so that in actual fact we were heartened by His help. Despite all the challenges of the heat, fires, and other exigencies we were triumphing in our hour-to-hour tasks.

Perhaps the most memorable day came when I decided to

take the bull by the horns, so to speak, and arrange for the transfer of all services to our new residence. So often this is a complicated job. One seems to run into one snarl after another. This time I was literally carried along swiftly from office to office with joyous ease. It was as if every clerk had been prepared in advance to expedite the transfer. They were so cordial, so cooperative, and so cheerful—all transactions were done in a day. I came home absolutely exhilarated.

Another astonishing and totally unexpected bonus, was the generous, lighthearted offer made by my son Rod to come across the Rocky Mountains to move us. It was such a generous gesture because first of all, it meant driving four hundred miles from his ranch to our place; and second, it meant arranging time off from his duties as chief consultant in one of Alberta's active oil fields.

In keeping with his usual efficient management, he and some friends showed up with two large trucks at 7:30 A.M. I had also rented a moving van in case of rain. It may seem hard to believe but by 11:30 A.M., we were completely moved into our new home and I could return the rented truck. I have never seen such a swift, smooth, sure move.

Cheri, with her skill and foresight had set up the kitchen the day before. At their own insistence, Rod's friends had come bearing homemade pies, delectable casseroles, and all the food for a full-blown first banquet in our home. What a happy celebration, overflowing with good will!

After a contented walk along the lake and a gentle interlude of relaxation, our movers left for home, and we snuggled into our nest. What a comfort!

That evening, as we reflected quietly upon the events of the year, it was transparently clear that our Father had arranged each move we had made. In His gentle, wondrous way He knew precisely when it was best for us to relocate. It was as if He had taken us each by the hand, like tiny tots, and calmly invited us to follow Him.

A profound peace enfolded us. We knew assuredly that not only had He prepared the way for us, but also He had prepared this place for us. Never, ever before had it been so simple to settle into new surroundings and be so elated at the loveliness of the new location.

Day after day, I discovered new hiking paths that led in various directions from our front door. There were quiet paths along the lake with wide views. There were trails down the river for miles. There were hikes in the hills. Close at hand were the green swards of a gorgeous rose garden, a golf course, and city parks across the sturdy footbridge. We were blessed, blessed, beyond our highest hopes.

An inner upwelling of joy, gratitude, peace, and praise arose to our Father. Surely, surely the lines of life had fallen for us in pleasant places. Thank you, Father!

Chapter Twenty-One

The Crash

The Bible studies were completed. They had been blessed in bountiful measure by our Father. Lives had been impacted by Christ in wondrous ways. His gracious Spirit had done a profound work among the people. Because of this, the youth pastor asked me to come to the church for just two more sessions with the young people on successive Friday evenings. I agreed to go.

This was not something I did as a rule. Especially because in our part of the country Friday nights are notorious for both wild and erratic drivers high on drugs and drunks who cruised the streets. Still, if there was serious service for the Master, I was prepared to carry out His wishes.

Before leaving home on the long drive, Ursula and I bowed our heads in earnest, childlike prayer. My humble request was very simple, direct, and sincere. "O my Father, this is Friday evening. You know all the great perils on the road from both drunks and druggies. I entreat you to preserve me as I travel. Thank you, Father!"

Cheri and I hugged each other in a fond farewell. I climbed in the car, expecting a gentle evening drive forty miles up the sun-dappled valley. To my delight the highway was almost clear of the usual heavy traffic. I had left early so there was no rush. The sweet-running Sonata cruised quietly along the lakeshore. Everything seemed so serene.

Suddenly a large, heavily loaded truck thundered out of a side road, hurtled through a stop sign, and crashed into me. For split seconds I was acutely aware of being safely enfolded by the very presence of Christ Himself. There was not any hint of panic. Nor was there an iota of pain.

Clearly, distinctively, I heard the splintering of glass. There was massive mangling of metal. The tires tore at the road. The two engines screamed as pipes burst. Then there was somber silence. I stepped out of the Sonata—now a wreck—unharmed and not even alarmed.

A car approaching from the opposite direction stopped. The lady driving it got out trembling like a leaf in the high wind. "I saw it all!" she gasped. "He just never stopped. Just plowed into you. I can't believe you are alive. And you're so calm!"

I asked her to come with me as a witness to see the truck driver, still in his cab. When I looked at him, he suddenly began to tremble, took a fit, and fell over on the seat.

I could only conclude that the young man was spaced-out on drugs. He wore a gruesome T-shirt depicting some sort of demonic creature, and his arms were covered with dark tattoos.

Just then other cars stopped to help. One man had a cellular phone so he quickly called for the police, an ambulance, and two tow trucks. He also let me call Ursula, asking her to contact the pastor and tell him that I could not come. She then bravely drove out to the scene of the wreck to pick me up.

When the Mountie arrived, he simply could not believe that I had come out of the crash unscathed. Over and over he questioned me closely to make sure I was not injured. Finally, the ambulance arrived to transport the truck driver to the hospital. The tow-truck owner took one quick look at my crumpled up car and grunted, "This one is a total wreck."

The police delayed my departure. A careful search of the truck gave hardly a single clue as to the owner. It was later determined the driver had no license, no registration, no insurance, and the truck was not his! Late that night the police called me at home to make sure I was not suffering from any aftershock. Again, the next morning, they asked me to report to their headquarters. All I could say was that I had been preserved in a remarkable manner.

The challenge that now confronted us was the formidable financial cost of replacing the beloved Sonata. It had been purchased about four years before at a special sale price, so its intrinsic value was not that great. Still it had been a superb car of high quality that had been a dream to drive. I had maintained it in immaculate condition. Now I was determined that the insurance people would have to repay me its proper replacement value, which they did, swiftly, smoothly, and without debate. To our utter astonishment the check was put in my hand within forty-eight hours of making the claim. What a stunning surprise!

The accident advisor assigned to my case had asked me pointedly, after filling out the forms, "Mr. Keller, have you any idea where you would have gone if you had been killed in this crash?"

My prompt, immediate response was, without a moment's hesitation, "I would be home, free, with my Father!"

He was delighted, for he, too, was a Christian. From then on he showed us great courtesy and unusual concern for the next car we should purchase. He highly recommended a Ford Taurus—a sturdy, well-built vehicle with many safety features including air bags, antilock brakes, steel in the doors, and so forth. Oddly enough, my son had suggested the same car to us as a safety precaution. We set out in search of one.

That very evening the local Ford dealer was holding a gala party for the public to introduce their new '95 models. I suggested to Cheri that we should go over and see if perchance they still had some '94 models of their Taurus cars at a reduced price.

When we arrived, everyone seemed to be in a festive mood. Their staff urged us to enjoy the drinks, but I made it clear that we had come in search of a car, not to party. Out on the huge sales lot we came across a brand new '94 Taurus, equipped just as we wished, and the right color.

It was parked in rather an unusual way, parallel to the highway. When I walked around it, it stunned me to see huge figures pasted on the side facing the road. It had been done to attract the attention of passing motorists. What startled me the most was the price, which was far, far below the regular cost of the vehicle.

We took it for a test drive. It seemed a solid, silent, responsive car. I was somewhat taken aback by its enormous power and imposing size. It was totally different to drive. However, we felt it was the car intended for us.

I told a salesman on duty that I would take it at the price pasted on the side. He became somewhat agitated and rushed off to see the manager. After a long wait, he returned rather sheepishly. Somehow, someone had made a serious mistake in putting the wrong price on the car.

Still, under the circumstances, they had no choice but to sell us the Taurus at this low price. I was elated! Once again our Father was caring for us in this time of trouble with remarkable arrangements of our affairs.

Despite the generous allowance made to us for the wrecked Sonata, plus the benefit of finding this new car at such a reasonable cost, a rather formidable difference in price still had to be made up. I have never been a man who paid high prices for prestigious vehicles. All my cars and trucks, bought and owned across years of hard driving have been modest in caliber and cost. They have been given great care as part of my personal responsibility, as one entrusted with their proper maintenance.

But I refuse to own cars for show. They are for service, and they must perform well to pay for their cost and upkeep. So, I did wonder if the Taurus was still too expensive despite all of its sturdy safety features.

Just two days later, exactly one week from the day of the crash, a very unusual letter came in our mail. A publisher wrote to apologize for an oversight in paying me properly for some work done several years before. Enclosed was a check, totally unexpected, that exactly covered all of the outstanding cost of the car. In fact, there was a small surplus of twenty dollars to pay for my first fill-up of gas! What fun! What joy!

Surely, surely our Father in His generous, gracious way had enabled us, His children, to triumph against trouble once more. Life with Him, even into advanced age, is an ongoing, astounding adventure. His presence, His peace, and His power are a distinct and dynamic aspect of our everyday affairs. His care and His concern for us are abundant and bountiful beyond mere belief.

In bringing this story to a close, there lies upon my spirit a compulsion to make several aspects of life with Christ very clear. It may help the reader to enter into a more intimate walk with our Father.

To just believe about God is sadly not enough.

This so-called casual belief must lead to knowing Him.

By knowing Christ it is understood that my entire life is opened to His entry and exposed to His scrutiny.

There is an actual exchange of our lives!

He enters mine. I also enter into His.

We become close companions and friends!

The acquaintance flourishes.

I trust Him. I follow Him.

He never fails me!

In love and loyalty I calmly do His bidding.

Then, and only then, there is no fear. He is here. All is well.

The same night of the crash, the young pastor spoke in my stead with intense earnestness. In that service a surprising group of young people gave themselves to Christ. It was well worth it all. Christ always, always triumphs against trouble!

Other Books by W. Phillip Keller

God Is My Delight
This widely read author examines his own personal relationship with the Trinity—God the Father, God the Son, and God the Holy Spirit—and shares his insights with those who are on the same journey he has traveled. Keller will give the reader a deeper desire to know God as Father, the Son as Friend, and the Holy Spirit as Counselor.
ISBN 0-8254-3051-8 256 pp. 14.95h

Joshua: Mighty Warrior and Man of Faith
The author of *A Shepherd Looks at Psalm 23* provides an interesting look at the successor to Moses and conqueror of Canaan. Keller examines the man and mission and gives practical insights for those in the Christian battle.
ISBN 0-8254-2999-4 184 pp. 9.99p

Outdoor Moments with God
An intimate and deeply spiritual recounting of moments spent with the Master—working in the yard, hiking in the mountains, or simply surveying some magnificent expanse of land and sky.
ISBN 0-8254-2996-x 192 pp. 10.99p

Sky Edge: Mountaintop Meditations
Out of the depths of his own heart, W. Phillip Keller shares with his readers insightful interludes illustrated with beautiful line drawings to convey in visual form the places they will visit with this fascinating author.
ISBN 0-8254-3052-6 208 pp. 9.99p

Songs of My Soul: Daily Devotions from the Writings of Phillip Keller, compiled by Al Bryant
Excerpts from the best-selling author's many books have been compiled into a beautiful daily devotional that displays the grandeur and goodness of God and our spiritual riches in Christ.
ISBN 0-8254-2995-1 256 pp. 11.99p

Strength of Soul: The Sacred Use of Time
Strength of soul and serenity of spirit are the vistas Phillip Keller opens to his readers in this wise, perceptive look at what it means to live a full, rewarding life not only in one's retirement years but throughout life.
ISBN 0-8254-2997-8 216 pp. 12.99h

Wonder O' the Wind
A companion volume to the popular spiritual biography *God Is My Delight.* Phillip Keller relives his trek back to Africa and eventually around the world in the Lord's service.
ISBN 0-8254-2998-6 244 pp. 11.99p